D0660871

Giving
—the sacred art

ALSO AVAILABLE IN
THE ART OF SPIRITUAL LIVING SERIES

Running—The Sacred Art:
Preparing to Practice
by Dr. Warren A. Kay
Foreword by Kristin Armstrong

Hospitality—The Sacred Art:
Discovering the Hidden Spiritual Power of
Invitation and Welcome
by Rev. Nanette Sawyer
Foreword by Rev. Dirk Ficca

Thanking and Blessing—The Sacred Art:
Spiritual Vitality through Gratefulness
by Jay Marshall, PhD
Foreword by Philip Gulley

Everyday Herbs in Spiritual Life:
A Guide to Many Practices
Written and Illustrated by Michael J. Caduto
Foreword by Rosemary Gladstar

The Sacred Art of Fasting:
Preparing to Practice
by Thomas Ryan, CSP

The Sacred Art of Bowing:
Preparing to Practice
by Andi Young

The Sacred Art of Chant:
Preparing to Practice
by Ana Hernández

The Sacred Art of Lovingkindness:
Preparing to Practice
by Rabbi Rami Shapiro
Foreword by Marcia Ford

Giving
—the sacred art

Creating a Lifestyle
of Generosity

LAUREN TYLER WRIGHT

Walking Together, Finding the Way ®
SKYLIGHT PATHS®
PUBLISHING
Woodstock, Vermont

Giving—The Sacred Art
Creating a Lifestyle of Generosity

2008 Quality Paperback Edition, First Printing
© 2008 by Lauren Tyler Wright

All rights reserved. No part of this book may be reproduced or transmitted in any form or by any means, electronic or mechanical, including photocopying, recording, or by any information storage and retrieval system, without permission in writing from the publisher.

For information regarding permission to reprint material from this book, please mail or fax your request in writing to SkyLight Paths Publishing, Permissions Department, at the address / fax number listed below, or e-mail your request to permissions@skylightpaths.com.

Translations used in the text are from the *Holy Bible: New Revised Standard Version* (Ontario: Hendrickson Publishers, 2004); *Tanakh: The Holy Scriptures* (Philadelphia: Jewish Publication Society, 1999); N.J. Dawood translation of the Koran (London: Penguin Classics, 2003).

Library of Congress Cataloging-in-Publication Data
Wright, Lauren Tyler, 1978–
Giving, the sacred art : creating a lifestyle of generosity / Lauren Tyler Wright.
    p. cm.— (The art of spiritual living series)
Includes bibliographical references.
ISBN-13: 978-1-59473-224-9 (pbk.)
ISBN-10: 1-59473-224-8 (pbk.)
1. Generosity. 2. Generosity—Religious aspects. I. Title.
BJ1533.G4W75 2008
205'.677—dc22

2008022480

10 9 8 7 6 5 4 3 2 1
Manufactured in the United States of America
Cover Design: Tim Holtz

SkyLight Paths Publishing is creating a place where people of different spiritual traditions come together for challenge and inspiration, a place where we can help each other understand the mystery that lies at the heart of our existence.

SkyLight Paths sees both believers and seekers as a community that increasingly transcends traditional boundaries of religion and denomination—people wanting to learn from each other, *walking together, finding the way.*

SkyLight Paths, "Walking Together, Finding the Way," and colophon are trademarks of LongHill Partners, Inc., registered in the U.S. Patent and Trademark Office.

Walking Together, Finding the Way®
Published by SkyLight Paths Publishing
A Division of LongHill Partners, Inc.
Sunset Farm Offices, Route 4, P.O. Box 237
Woodstock, VT 05091
Tel: (802) 457-4000   Fax: (802) 457-4004
www.skylightpaths.com

To Hugh and Carol Tyler

Mom and Dad, you modeled generosity and raised your most precious crumbcrusher and rugrat to do the same.
I love you both ... big time.

CONTENTS

INTRODUCTION:
GIVING AS A SACRED ART?

giving—voluntarily transferring something from one person to another without expecting compensation
—Merriam-Webster Online Dictionary, www.m-w.com

GIVING IS A PRACTICE FOR ALL

The practice of giving comes in all forms—offering a smile, picking out a necktie for Dad, reducing debt in third-world countries. When practiced consistently and intentionally, giving can become a spiritual discipline and, even more, a sacred art. When we practice giving regularly and understand that our motivation has some connection outside of ourselves, we have the opportunity to radically transform our lives, the life of another person, even the lives of entire communities. This sacred opportunity is open to anyone—parents, business executives, retirees, students, clergy. This book is dedicated to exploring the many dimensions of the practice of giving, from the little acts that seem pointless to the big acts that seem impossible. It's about creating an entire lifestyle of generosity. This transformation will help you connect to other people; it will relieve stress from the daily worries of your life; it will open you up to encounters with the Sacred. Most important, creating a lifestyle of generosity will allow you to do good in this world. Your giving will have a ripple effect; it will be passed on to other people, other families, other communities, other countries, other generations. Your giving will change the world.

The transforming power of any spiritual discipline comes with regular practice, but the rewards inherent in the practice can be reaped from the beginning. You don't have to become an expert before it becomes worthwhile. I say this because giving sometimes gets put off as a practice to be taken up "later" or "when we have more money" or "when we're older." But procrastinating only robs you of the chance to experience the joys of giving now. And giving is a timely practice. As many of us are becoming more and more isolated thanks to long commutes in our cars, private entertainment on our MP3 players, or the ability to telecommute from home, giving offers us a way to enhance relationships and create community.

The topic of philanthropy has recently made a splash in pop culture with politicians writing books on the subject, feel-good reality shows popping up left and right, and celebrities writing checks and acting as ambassadors on almost every issue. All of this is good news, but it also makes me excited to share the insights in this book that you will not find in mainstream sources. What they don't offer is an explicit invitation for each and every person on the planet to participate in giving. Instead, they trick us into thinking that giving is only for the rich, the famous, the powerful; and conversely that receiving is only for the dying, the critically ill, or the destitute. They leave the rest of us to sit back and watch; we are simply observers to the transaction. But the truth is that we don't have to sit at home watching another home-makeover show; each and every one of us can participate fully as both a giver and a receiver.

Take me, for instance. Born in South Carolina to a stay-at-home mom and a local butcher, I was a typical American girl. But my parents modeled giving in ways they probably weren't even aware of. Mom made sure she was home every afternoon when my brother and I got home from school to make us a snack, ask about our day, and help with homework; Dad offered a listening ear to his employees and slipped them cash when life was hard; Mom once heard about thieves breaking into a handful of my friends' cars and replaced all the items that were taken; Dad paid for kids' scooters at the church but didn't want anyone to know it was him. My parents are not rich. Their names do not appear in donor lists or on plaques. They do not claim many, if any, donations for tax purposes. But I learned from them what it means to live generously. I have also had the privilege to grow up with a brother who is unlike any sibling this planet has ever seen. In grade school, I remember watching him attend the funeral of a classmate's father. Afterward, as he greeted his friend, he removed his cross necklace and placed it around her neck. He loved that necklace and had never let it out of his sight, until that day. On another occasion, Christian was performing with his band at an outdoor concert on a frigid night. The event sponsor had brought them chili for dinner. Christian hadn't eaten all day and was starving, but there was a homeless man nearby, so Christian skipped dinner that night so that man could eat.

While I have many formal credentials in the fields of religion and philanthropy, I am most thankful for what my family has taught me about giving. They taught me as a child to enjoy giving, and I think that is why I'm writing this book today. That's not to say the more official influences haven't played a part. A bachelor's degree in religious studies from Furman University got me started. A master of divinity degree from Duke Divinity School came next. Then I spent time working at the Lake Institute on Faith & Giving, a program of the Center on Philanthropy at Indiana University. I now have the pleasure of speaking to people from all across the country about faith and giving—leading seminars for local churches, community foundations, and denominational groups; consulting with nonprofit organizations and local churches. And no matter where I go or who I speak to, one thing is always true: giving is for *all* people—all ages, all stages of life, all socioeconomic states.

WHY IS GIVING SO PROFOUNDLY TRANSFORMATIVE?

Giving is profoundly transformative because it requires two people or entities—a giver and a receiver, *both* of whom are affected by the act of giving. In the seminars I lead on the subject of giving, time and again I encounter participants who are under the impression that when a gift is given, the good stuff happens only to the recipient, not the giver. But that's just not true. The act of giving is a source of blessing for both parties. A wise Chinese proverb says: "A bit of fragrance always clings to the hand that gives roses." Generosity can give you joy, it can remind you of the purpose of life, it can give you a greater connection with the vast expanse of humanity, and it can give you the power to change the world. You, as the giver, have the opportunity to make positive changes in your own life by giving.

I'll give you one example of how the sustained practice of giving cultivated a positive change in my life. During seminary, I was easily annoyed by strangers—the cashier who talks to her coworker during our entire transaction, the driver who throws bags of litter out his window, the mother who lets her child run wild throughout the store. So, I decided to do something about it. I made a conscious decision to acknowledge the people I encountered during the day. By simply asking, "How's your day going?" my hope was to transform how I saw strangers. By giving them my attention, my smile, a moment of my time, I got to understand a little bit of why they are the way they are, which kept me from getting annoyed.

At first, the practice felt awkward, and each time I approached a stranger I had to remind my introverted self that this practice was, in fact, a good idea. But over time, it became natural. I no longer had to make an intentional decision to engage with strangers; the practice of recognizing "the other" became so much of a habit that my perception of strangers has been transformed. If someone seems in a bad mood, I now cannot help but look them in the eye and wonder what keeps them up at night. Do they have an aging parent who is dying? Do they feel overwhelmed at work? Do they suffer from an addiction but not want to tell anyone? Seeing a person this way, rather than just as someone irritated with me, took time and took many intentional, "How's your day?" moments. Now I am able to avoid getting stressed when a stranger cuts me off on the road, or assuming I've done something wrong when the stranger handing me my drive-through order appears mute.

I've been sad to discover that, despite the universal popularity of gift receiving, gift giving is not such a hit with the majority of people. Unless, of course, you count giving to yourself as a form of gift giving—that practice is all the rage. L'Oreal cosmetics is memorable for their slogan, "Because you're worth it." Burger King famously tells you to "have it your way." One local bank has a slogan on their website that reads, "It really *is* all about you." We are a culture of "me first, you last." Now, don't get me wrong, I often find ways to be generous to myself; my guilty pleasures happen to be shoes and handbags. But as exhilarating as a new pair of heels can be, the practice of giving is much more gratifying when somebody else is the receiver. And for that reason, this book is an alternative voice amid the chant of "consume" and "take" that our culture shouts at us. Loudly, I call back, "Give and be generous!" Giving reorders our priorities, in sometimes surprisingly subversive ways. Practicing the sacred art of giving helps replace the narrow perspective of "me" with an expansive view of "we."

This is not to say that we're always on the giving end. How we receive is just as important as how we give. One of my favorite wedding presents is a small statue of two people facing each other. It is clear that one figure is giving to the other figure, but it is not clear which is which. Both figures in the statue are giver and receiver, and there is no delineation between where one role starts and the other role stops. The statue is a reminder that receiving a gift is just as important as giving a gift; it is a reciprocal relationship. In Judaism, giving is understood as a relationship between God, receiver, and giver, and the positions are ranked in that order. In many faith traditions, we find similar admonitions to treat the recipient of a gift with respect and to recognize that donors benefit as much or more than recipients. According to one rabbinic teaching, "More than the householder does for the poor, the poor does for the householder" (R. Yehoshua, *Vayikra Rabba* 34:8).

Receiving a gift can be more difficult than you expect. For some, accepting a gift somehow implies that they are incomplete. For others, it creates a sense of indebtedness to the giver. We may not want to admit dependence on other people, but learning how to accept gifts makes us better givers because we know what it is like to be on the opposite end of the exchange. Moreover, learning how to accept gifts opens us up to experience the joys that other people have to offer us.

I remember the first time I let my mother-in-law bring me dinner. I had just moved to a new city, my belongings were still in boxes, and I was in the midst of trying to plan a wedding in another state. Time and again, Ann offered to bring me dinner, but I continually refused her offers because I felt like that was too much to ask of her, and that as a grown woman I should at least be able to manage dinner. One night the anxiety of a new city, a new home, and wedding plans was too much, and I finally said yes to her offer. As she rang the doorbell and walked in with an entire tray of food (small vase and flower included), I could see on her face how much it meant to her to provide this gift. Somehow, seeing her happiness freed me to enjoy the gift and not worry about the time it had taken her to prepare it, or what she might think of me as a stressed-out bride-to-be.

Learning how to accept that meal allowed me to fully experience the gift she was offering. The German writer Johann Wolfgang von Goethe (1749–1832) wrote: "One would give generous alms if one had the eyes to see the beauty of a cupped receiving hand."

In its healthiest form, the sacred art of giving is about relationship. When we give and when we receive, we are reminded that we need other people to survive. Even the richest people in the world have needs that only another human can meet. No matter how substantial their gifts are to others, they too need to be the recipient of gifts. We are all givers and all receivers; these are not two distinct groups of people. While some have plenty of money to give away and others don't have enough to provide for their own needs, even the poorest of the poor can offer a smile as an expression of generosity. The Prophet Muhammad said, "Even a smile is charity." No matter what the balance of our savings account or the scope of our talents, all of us have something to give.

When we give within relationship, the transferring of an object from one person to another becomes transformative, not just transactional. Transactions form the fabric of our lives in our free-market capitalist system, and this influences the way that we think about giving—it becomes one more simple transaction, one less item on the to-do list. So often we limit our giving to transactional exchanges such as writing a check for an organization or bringing a few canned goods to a collection box. While giving money or objects in this way does provide some level of reward, the deeper transformational power of giving is activated when we give within the context of an actual relationship. Giving within relationship can be revolutionary because we are connecting with another person, and thereby connecting with God.

THE ROLE OF RELIGION

The various spiritual traditions I discuss in these pages play a dual role in this book. First, they provide a descriptive paradigm or framework for describing these various practices. Second, they offer prescriptive challenges to give us fresh opportunities to enrich our practice of giving.

When asked why they give, people cite any number of reasons: seeing the joy on a friend's face as she unwraps a present; wanting to share God's blessing with others; wanting all children to have sufficient material possessions. Some believe that "it's just the right thing to do," and others give as a response to holy commandments in the Bible or the sacred texts of their faith. Though specific motivations may vary, a common thread that weaves its way through many responses is religion. Statistics bear out a correlation, and possible causation, between a giver's faith and the type, size, and frequency of their giving.

The connection between faith and giving is more than anecdotal. Research shows that religious people are arguably the most generous people in the world.[1] Furthermore, religious institutions are the primary benefactor of philanthropic action.[2] In other words, religious people do most of the giving and religious institutions receive most of the gifts. People of faith have discovered the rich and powerful effect giving can have on our lives. People of faith have experienced how the practice of giving can offer meaning to life and transform both the giver and the receiver. Within the context of faith, giving can be elevated beyond charity or good deeds; it can become a deliberate spiritual practice, even a sacred art. Hence the title of this book: *Giving—The Sacred Art.*

It is also helpful to see religion as a prescriptive challenge for the practice of giving. Our spiritual life, our religion, our faith, is much more than what we claim to believe and uphold in times of prayer, meditation, and reflection. It is as much, if not more, about how we live and what we practice. Our faith influences every aspect of life—all the way down to what we do with the dollar bills in our wallet. We can try to separate how we understand God and what we do with a quarter, but in the end such attempts fail because our understanding of the Sacred influences what we do with our time, our money, and our possessions. Attempting to compartmentalize our faith and our practices only leads to conflict within our soul. Instead, we should try to see the practice of giving as a way for us to live out our religious beliefs.

While I write as a Christian, my faith is deeply enriched by the teachings of my brothers and sisters who practice other traditions. In this book we will look at examples of giving from a variety of traditions (Christianity, Judaism, Islam, Buddhism, Hinduism, and others) in order to explore creative ways in which you can experience the joy and richness of the sacred art of giving—perhaps in ways that you have never considered before. As you read, receive the gifts of insight from other faiths that may be unfamiliar. Each tradition brings to the table a beautiful history of sacred texts, stories, and experiences, and each faith contributes to the intricate landscape of religious giving with a beautiful assortment of expressions: stewardship, almsgiving, *zakat* (alms tax), *sadaqah* (voluntary charity), *dana* (giving), charity, *chesed* (loving-kindness), *tzedakah* (righteous giving), *tikkun olam* (repairing the world). As I write, I imagine this wide variety of religious perspectives engaging in dialogue, not debate. While we may disagree on a host of ideologies, we can all sit around the table of generosity and share our understandings of this common practice. And in doing so, I have a feeling we will discover that our spiritual journeys are more alike than we may have thought. In the end, it is up to you to determine your own faith journey, but I hope you will take advantage of those walking the road alongside you.

Not only does the spiritual practice of giving transcend religious persuasions, it also crosses all ages, races, and socioeconomic levels. This book is for everyone: clergy and laity, rich and poor, old and young. I am grateful to God that our ability to participate in spiritual practices is not based on our weight, whether we've been to college, or the kind of car we drive.

As you read, each chapter will take you through different ways to understand and practice giving: giving as worship, giving as stewardship, giving as holy obligation, giving as redemption, giving as charity, and giving as justice. My hope is that you will examine your own life for opportunities to engage in this sacred practice. Rest assured, I have no ulterior motive, no hidden agenda for you to give to my favorite charity. Instead, I have a sincere desire to help people of all faiths experience the joy of giving. I hope that this book will create a safe space for you to discover the delight that can be found in this ancient practice.

While I hope to inspire those who do not consider themselves persons of faith, it is important to acknowledge that this book is about the sacred art of giving. Why the *sacred* art of giving? What makes religious giving different from secular giving? Secular giving seeks to strengthen civil society through the power of humans. Sacred giving seeks to strengthen God's creation through the power of God manifested in humans. Philanthropy not tied to a practice of faith is a good act, but it is not the topic of this work. Instead, we are embarking on a journey to explore and experience the joy and fulfillment that comes through the sacred art of giving.

GIVING IS ABOUT MONEY—AND MORE

This book will provide you with a wide range of ways to be generous, but we will spend a good amount of time on how to be generous specifically with our money. Why money? Because money is often the most difficult area of generosity to practice. It can also be the most accessible way for people to begin this practice. And money is typically the thing that we like to talk about least when discussing ways to be generous. For these reasons, money will take up more time in our discussions than any other single form of giving. But as you read, you will also be given plenty of ideas for nonmonetary ways to practice generosity. Giving is certainly not limited to money alone.

Many of us either lack a spiritual imagination for what nonmonetary acts of giving look like or push giving to the very edge of our spiritual imaginations. Diluting the practice of giving to money alone deprives us of a rich variety of giving experiences. Adopting a lifestyle of generosity is about more than writing checks; it is an entire way of life. It is about how we look at other people and react. It is about how we spend our weekends. It is about how we use our talents. While opening our wallets is a great start, we are called to *embody* generosity. We are called to act. We are called to give of our *selves*.

Here are just a few examples of giving that do not involve money:

- Give time—volunteer at a nonprofit organization
- Give hospitality—open your home to other people for a meal
- Give energy—pray or meditate on the needs of others
- Give comfort or space—surrender your seat on the bus or train to allow someone else a place to sit
- Give your body—donate blood or make plans to donate your organs[3]
- Give possessions—pass on your clothes and housewares to an organization that can redistribute them through thrift shops
- Give forgiveness—forgive those who have hurt you

The opportunities to practice giving are endless.

GIVING AS A LIFESTYLE OF GENEROSITY

A lifestyle of generosity is bigger than an annual fifty cents in the bell-ringer's red kettle at Christmas. For that matter, it's bigger than any number of behavioral modifications merely strung together. It's something much more nuanced, integrated, and mysterious. And if you are willing, you can experience the transformative effects of this practice. Living generously, in its most complete form, involves knowing people, sharing in the mundane parts of their lives, touching them, forming relationships with them, knowing their weaknesses.

My husband, Brent, had a profound experience with the organization Big Brothers Big Sisters. As a college student, Brent was a big brother to twelve-year-old Dustin, a boy big for his age and lacking many friends. The time Brent and Dustin spent together over three years wasn't particularly profound, but when Brent's father was killed in a commercial airline crash, Dustin attended the funeral, and this is one of the few memories that still sticks with Brent. Dustin and his mother did not have their own transportation, so they found someone to drive them the hour's journey to the affluent mega-church on the north side of town. The expedition took so much effort that Dustin and his mother actually missed the service entirely. As it ended and the family processed out of the church, these two strangers entered—empty-handed, casually dressed, and tardy—but present. Over five hundred people filled the space that day, but it was the presence of one young boy that still touches Brent the most, even ten years later. The relationship between Dustin and Brent created a space for profound transformational giving.

I was once quoted at a conference for saying, "Giving is not for sissies." I said it off the cuff, but looking back, I really agree with myself. Living generously is a tough and costly practice. It's not a weekend project with step-by-step instructions obtained on the Internet. In *Acts of Compassion*, Princeton sociologist Robert Wuthnow writes that modern charitable giving "allows us to carve up our caring into little chunks that require only a level of giving that does not conflict with our needs and interests as individuals."[4] Living generously means giving a large portion of our possessions and wealth to others for the sake of making the world better. It means being strategic about what we have and what we do with what we have. It might mean sacrificial living. Living generously means always asking the question, "What can I do with my life for others *today*?" Don't get overwhelmed and try to save the world in an afternoon or you'll be bound for failure. Just take one step at a time.

ONE STEP AT A TIME

A lifestyle of any kind is not made up of an isolated act. Instead, a lifestyle is comprised of hundreds of like-minded acts fitted together, transforming the sum of the parts into the whole. Recently, I have become a fan of mosaics. These artistic creations can encompass entire walls, floors, or ceilings, and yet they are created one tiny square at a time. Just as a mosaic involves countless individual tiles, a lifestyle of generosity involves numerous daily acts of generosity. When giving is practiced as a lifestyle, instead of as a few isolated events, the glue that holds these tiny tiles together is something mysterious. For me, it is my Christian faith. For you, it may be something different. Regardless of the type of glue you use, the reality is that many of us only attach a tile onto our mosaic of generosity during the holidays or when there is a crisis.

Calling the practice of giving an "art" implies many things. No two pieces of art are ever the same; nuances of color, shape, and texture form the beauty of each piece. Likewise, no two styles of giving are ever identical. While one person might feel that God is asking him to give all of his possessions away and live among the poor, another person might feel led to amass a great deal of money and leverage her wealth for the sake of other people. Each style is equally valid, holy, and beautiful.

The art of giving looks different for different people and can even vary over time within the same person depending on circumstances. Just as there are no step-by-step instructions for how to create an artistic masterpiece, the art of giving does not offer a list of regimented steps to follow. There is no one answer to questions such as, "Why should I give?" "What should I give?" "When should I give?" "To whom should I give?" and "How much should I give?" The answers will vary from person to person and from experience to experience, much like religious expression. Generosity, like personhood itself, is beautifully aesthetic in all its varieties. Giving is a spiritual practice that is nuanced and adaptable. Accepting this diversity is freeing because you do not have to compare your generosity to the way other people choose to practice giving. Twelfth- and thirteenth-century Italian monk Francis of Assisi, who was noted for his gentleness toward all creation, and modern rock star Bono, outspoken lead singer for the rock band U2 and one of *Time* magazine's "Persons of the Year" in 2005, are examples of noted philanthropists, but the manner in which each lives or lived his lifestyle of generosity could hardly be more different. You too can discern how you will create your own lifestyle of generosity.

Like the development of an artistic masterpiece, giving as a spiritual discipline is a journey or process. To be clear, when I say "practice," I don't mean an occasional act of charity. I mean an intentional way of being that spans the course of a lifetime. The creation of art happens over the course of many steps, and in this process beauty can be found. The creation of a piece of art is not just a means to an end but is an end in itself. In the same way, the sacred art of giving produces meaning and delight in each step along the journey. We cannot simply "achieve" a lifestyle of generosity, reap the benefits, and check it off our list. Rather, we learn the practice of generosity while we walk our faith journey, step by step, finding joy and fulfillment in each segment, and always seeking to grow through various spiritual practices. This is great news because it means we do not have to "master" the practice before we experience its rewards.

Just like any spiritual practice, giving is something that can be integrated into our lives. When we create a *lifestyle* of giving, not just participating in a whirlwind of giving one weekend and then dropping the practice, our lives can become continuously filled with the blessings that come from this spiritual practice. Creating a lifestyle of generosity is more than just behavioral modifications; it is seeing the world differently every day. When we are able to change our paradigm and see each moment and aspect of our life as an opportunity to be generous, we open ourselves up to experience the rich rewards that occur through sustained giving. Sacred giving can occur in the mundane grocery-store moments of everyday life, not just in those headline-grabbing, once-in-a-lifetime major financial gifts. While the goal is to create a lifestyle, you have to start somewhere. Don't be afraid to start small. It's the intentionality and regularity of the act that is most important, not the size of the gift. Think of it as a mosaic of small practices that, before you know it, add up to a lifestyle. Taking small, consistent steps now is far better than waiting until the "right time." Just take the next faithful step.

WHAT YOU WILL FIND IN THIS BOOK

This book will give you a framework for understanding the philosophy behind this spiritual discipline, a variety of perspectives and resources from religious traditions, and a tool-kit for putting into practice this lifestyle choice. As you read, you will notice that the chapters are organized by six different motivations for giving: worship, stewardship, obligation, redemption, charity, and justice. I have placed them in order of what I consider increasingly dramatic potential. As I mentioned earlier, the act of giving is a source of blessing for the receiver and the giver. Different forms of giving produce different results that range from more personal joy to the opportunity to change the world. No matter the form, however, all experiences of giving provide an opportunity to participate with God in divine work.

Here is a preview of each chapter.

1. Giving can be an act of worship. For example, most faith communities collect money as an act of worship. Giving as worship offers you the chance to live out your gratitude for the gift of life.

2. Giving can be an act of stewardship. For example, giving gently used household items to a thrift store rather than throwing them away is one way you might steward the possessions you have been entrusted with. Giving as stewardship yields freedom and contentment when dealing with possessions and wealth.

3. Giving can be an act of obligation. For example, many Jewish people give money away out of a duty called *tzedakah* (righteous giving). Obligatory giving shapes the givers' identity in life-giving ways.

4. Giving can be an act of redemption. For example, when I gave my old car away rather than selling it, I redeemed its value. Giving as redemption restores money and moves it from a profane to sacred object.

5. Giving can be an act of charity, such as giving a meal to a homeless family. Giving as charity transforms your point of view and makes room for you to encounter the Sacred.

6. Giving can be an act of justice, such as participating in a peace rally. Giving as justice offers you the chance to tap into the work of God in this world.

By the end of this book, you will be ready start your unique journey of living generously thanks to an eclectic collection of resources and numerous variations of the practice. Actually, you have already started. You are reading this book and exploring the topic of giving. Plus, your purchase of this book has helped a good cause. Every dollar I make from this book is going to the United Nations World Food Programme. So, thank you.

A NOTE ON THE TEXT

The following translations were used throughout the book, unless otherwise indicated: *Holy Bible: New Revised Standard Version*, *Tanakh: The Holy Scriptures*, and N.J. Dawood's translation of the Koran.

CHAPTER ONE

GIVING AS WORSHIP

Responding to God's Generosity with Joyful Gratitude

worship—*reverence offered a divine being or supernatural power; an act of expressing such reverence*
—Merriam-Webster Online Dictionary, www.m-w.com

One activity that faiths across the globe share—whatever their differences may be—is worship. But worship is a big topic. It is many things to many people and can look very different from tradition to tradition. It may involve praying, chanting, singing, or extended periods of intentional silence. It may involve kneeling, listening to a sermon, or dancing passionately. It may even involve kissing a sacred text, as in one faith community I visited, or processing around a sacred space with incense or a holy object.

Even within a single religion, worship may look radically different from place to place. If you visit a Presbyterian church on a Sunday morning, you are likely to experience a staid, punctual, and orderly service, nothing like the hand-waving, dynamic worship experience you will likely experience if you visit a Pentecostal church. Both are Christian worship services, but the styles of worship are different.

What's more, the motivations for worship are as varied as the styles of worship. Some worship to receive comfort or guidance.

Others worship to affirm their beliefs and experience God. Still others worship because it is a duty or expectation.

And yet, within the many forms worship can take, there are fundamental similarities that make worship, *worship*. One essential element of worship is that it is an intentional expression of reverence toward God, however a tradition might conceive of God. Another is that worship involves feelings of joyful gratitude. Sometimes that means expressing the joy and gratefulness worshipers already feel for the gifts they have received. Sometimes worshipers hope their worship experience will *generate* feelings of joyful gratitude in the form of solace, serenity, or even ecstasy as they encounter the presence of God, either alone or in the presence of like-minded believers.

The topic of this book—giving—has many similarities to worship. In fact, when you give with intention, you may find that giving is a transformational *form* of worship that expresses reverence for God, generates joyful gratitude, and leads you to a closer relationship with the Sacred. This might be a radical idea to some, but in fact this wisdom is rooted in the sacred scriptures of many faiths:

> "Charity is equal in importance to all other commandments combined."
>
> (Talmud *Baba Batra* 9a)

> "He will give (charity) and he wants others to give—he is truly pious."
>
> (Talmud *Mishnah Abot* 5:13 IV D)

> "You shall never be truly righteous until you give in alms what you dearly cherish. The alms you give are known to God."
>
> (Qur'an *Al-Imran* 3:92)

"The righteous man is he who ... though he loves it dearly, gives away his wealth to kinsfolk, to orphans, to the destitute, to the traveler in need and to beggars, and for the redemption of captives."

(Qur'an *Al-Baqarah* 2:177)

"Remembering the words of the Lord Jesus, for he himself said, 'It is more blessed to give than to receive.'"

(Acts 20:35)

"Then the king will say to those at his right hand, 'Come, you that are blessed by my Father, inherit the kingdom prepared for you from the foundation of the world; for I was hungry and you gave me food, I was thirsty and you gave me something to drink, I was a stranger and you welcomed me, I was naked and you gave me clothing, I was sick and you took care of me, I was in prison and you visited me.... Truly I tell you, just as you did it to one of the least of these who are members of my family, you did it to me.'"

(Matthew 25:34–36, 40)

"On the high ridge of heaven he stands exalted, yea, to the Gods he goes, the liberal giver. The streams, the waters flow for him with fatness: to him this guerdon ever yields abundance."

(*Rig Veda* 1.125.5)

"The Buddha said: 'When you see someone practicing the Way of giving, aid him joyously, and you will obtain vast and great blessings.' A shramana asked: 'Is there an end to those blessings?' The Buddha said: 'Consider the flame of a single lamp. Though a hundred thousand people come and light their own lamps from it so that they can cook their food and ward off the darkness, the first lamp remains the same as before. Blessings are like this, too.'"

(*Tripitaka Sutra* 10)

"'If I give this to others, what shall I have to enjoy?' Such self-cherishing is the mind of a hungry spirit. 'If I enjoy this, what shall I have to give to others?' Such cherishing of others is the mind of the enlightened ones."

(*Shantideva's Guide to the Bodhisattva's Way of Life* 8.125)

Giving in all its forms, both financial and otherwise, can be an act of worship by virtue of its unique power to remind us that life itself, with all its ups and downs, all its struggles and heartaches and victories, is fundamentally a gift from God.

WHY SEEING LIFE AS A GIFT IS IMPORTANT

Every day we are bombarded with the message that whatever we want, we actually deserve. This seductive message of entitlement places each of us at the center of the universe, and you might think it would be quite empowering. Who wouldn't want to be at the center, where no want is untended, no craving is unfulfilled?

And yet, buying into that message doesn't really satisfy us. As an antidote, we turn to another set of messages that promises that the accumulation of things will make us happy. But when the novelty of the latest gadget wears off, we are told that the newer, sleeker, faster-processing gadget is the key to our happiness. And so we enter into a shiny and strangely empty circle of unfulfilled promises for more, more, more.

When we adopt the alternative paradigm that life and everything we already possess is a gift, not a right, we turn the narratives of entitlement on their head. Craig Gay, associate professor of interdisciplinary studies at Regent College in Vancouver, British Columbia, in his book *Cash Values,* writes, "The single most subversive and ultimately redemptive idea that we can set loose within the capitalist world today is the simple recognition that life is a gift.... We respond to God's gracious gift of the world by simply being gracious and generous with one another."[1]

I love Gay's use of *subversive* to describe this paradigm shift. It frees us from our ties to the powerful cultural narratives of discontent and scarcity and allows us to experience joyful gratitude with what we already have, what is right in front of us, which is often more than we already need.

Worship reorders our values and our priorities by helping us fasten our vision on the eternal, on that which transcends our small egos. Likewise, giving in all its forms helps us to reorder our everyday perceptions that keep "me" and what is "mine" at the center of the universe. By giving, we release our desire to hold desperately to what is in our hands and find that we are left with open palms and a mind no longer distracted by clinging to stuff. This posture of open hands and open mind, in turn, spurs further generous giving and helps us to see through the cultural clutter to the deep interconnectedness we all share.

The pattern of joyful gratitude and giving that I'm discussing doesn't have to tackle big topics or involve big actions. It can be tough to reconcile thankfulness with the realities of debt, grief, and illness. The key is to be intentional about noticing moments of God's generosity and grace in our day—that we woke up healthy, that we had a good night's sleep, that we avoided a traffic accident.

There are a number of techniques that can help you remember your intent throughout the day. Television host Oprah Winfrey made popular the ritual of keeping a daily record of things you are grateful for in a gratitude journal. Another trick is to begin the day with five rubber bands on your right wrist and to move one band to the left wrist every time you recognize things you are grateful for as the day progresses. Even casually meditating on your gratefulness throughout the day can serve as a catalyst for living out a life of generosity.

For example, as I sit and write in a coffee shop today, I am mindful of the gifts in my life. My husband is sitting in the chair beside me, giving up his plans this afternoon because I wanted company while I write. I am drinking coffee that I bought with the cash in my wallet, cash that I took out of an ATM earlier today without fear that the account balance would drop too low. Tonight I will return home in a safe and reliable vehicle, and I will sleep comfortably, not fearing for my safety or distracted by the noises of neighbors. On a lighter note, I am grateful for the clean and folded stack of laundry my husband took care of yesterday, the chocolate chip cookie that awaits me on the kitchen counter, and the forecast that the sun will be out tomorrow. My awareness of all these gifts from God leads to a specific response, which will be to leave a big tip for the waitress when I leave, not because it's expected of me but because I feel relaxed, joyful, and grateful for everything I have already. We set off a sacred chain reaction when we live out of thanksgiving for the abundance of God; gratitude spurs generosity.

But is all this an act of worship? Inasmuch as this kind of thinking is an intentional attitude of joyful gratitude for the God-given gifts of life that surround us constantly, it is. And so we have circled back to the deep wisdom found in the world's great religious traditions—that giving, especially monetary giving, can be a potent act of worship. Let's explore this in more depth.

GIVING MONEY AS WORSHIP

It's funny how giving money in particular has such potency.

A few months ago, I encountered a man in the bread aisle of the grocery store who was in need of change to buy a loaf of bread. He was deaf and could only point and mouth the words of his request. At first I shook my head to the right and left because I had no change. But then I thought, "For goodness sake, Lauren, you have no coins but you do have bills." I caught his attention, gave him a dollar bill and was taken aback when this stranger embraced me with a hug and a barely audible "thank you."

Around that same time, I happened to be dealing with the sudden death of someone close. I was having a hard time comprehending the loss—it was a sad and confusing time. What I discovered in the store that day was that somehow, giving that man a buck for bread helped change things for me. Giving money to him got me out of my own skin—only for a minute, perhaps, but long enough to help me glimpse a larger perspective beyond the boundaries of my own sorrow. When that man took my dollar with a grateful smile and then hugged me, I realized I had been a catalyst for joyful gratitude in *his* life. This, in turn, helped *me* remember the things in my life that I believe are gifts from God, for which I am grateful. In this way, the simple act of giving a dollar bill to a stranger was a small, but powerful, act of worship in my life.

Usually, when a stranger approaches me for money, my first reaction is one of suspicion. What is he going to use it for? If I don't give him any money, will he become confrontational? Should I lie and say I don't have any money, even though he just saw me coming from the ATM? Is it ever really true that I don't have any money to give when I drive a new Volvo?

Indeed, when it comes to giving money, we all seem to exhibit a peculiar kind of reluctance to part with it. If a neighbor asked you to spend an afternoon helping him move some furniture, you might not be thrilled about giving up part of your weekend, but you would likely put in a few hours just to be a good neighbor. But if the same neighbor knocked on your door and asked for a hundred dollars to tide him over "just until payday," well, you can probably already hear the excuses rising about why you can't, or won't, lend the money.

The point is not whether or not you should give your neighbor the hundred dollars—that's up to you. The point is to illustrate the innate power money has in our lives and the things we'll do to get it and keep it. The power that money has to comfort us, to motivate us, and even to define us, is what makes giving money such a potent form of worship. When we give away money, we also give away the power it represents. We give away the fear that we won't have enough money, the fear that our generosity will somehow be taken advantage of.

We also give up a measure of control when we worship. When we express reverence toward a supernatural being, we acknowledge that our lives are not our own. As those in the addiction community regularly affirm through twelve-step programs, we are powerless on our own, but a power greater than ourselves can restore us to sanity.[2]

A Word about Expectations and Motives

My experience in the bread aisle at the grocery store was simple and dramatic, at least for me in that moment. But the joy associated with giving of all types is not necessarily, or even usually, so straightforward; rarer still is it a sentimental, exuberant bliss that causes us to forget that we have a mortgage bill due or that we've put on a few extra pounds over the winter. It's not like a drug-induced high. The joyful gratitude I'm talking about is much more subtle and complex. It's not a happiness that overrides other emotions; it's a gladness that sits alongside our pain. The joy we get from being generous is deep, because it grounds us in our connectedness to others, in our common humanity. It is a framework on which to hang other emotions because we become connected to the essential meaning of life when we give.

This is important to note because media images, which profoundly influence our expectations, often strip joy of its deepest meanings and replace it with a strange, unattainable state of happiness. Television commercials, one after another, promise a blissed-out state of euphoria, where the house is forever immaculate and the kids are all smiles, if only you use this detergent or that toilet paper. This oddly unrealistic vision passes for joy, or at least happiness, in our culture.

Movies that portray volunteering time with the elderly, for example, usually paint it as a docile activity that is nothing but laughing over hot tea, putting together puzzles, and knitting scarves while the youthful volunteer receives bits of sage advice from the gracefully aging senior. They tend to leave out the rest of the story, which often includes sponge baths, dementia, incontinence, and the like. And yet the combination of encountering the negatives and still caring for others is what makes giving valuable in the first place. Part of the true joy we receive from giving comes from creating a relationship with another person; and relationships are always messy. It is therefore important to be aware of these misleading cultural images of joy, lest we become discouraged that our own efforts at giving don't seem to measure up to our expectations.

Another key factor that we should cautiously consider in practicing giving is our motivation. Joyful gratitude can easily be confused with other feelings. When we give to someone, we sometimes have the opportunity to see how much or how little that person may possess. And when we compare that to the money and possessions we have, we often feel good because we're not as bad off as they are.

Looking down on those we give to and feeling good only because we happen to be in a more privileged state than they are is dangerous. It is a kind of modern-day noblesse oblige that misses the genuine experience of joyful gratitude. Instead of helping us transcend our own boundaries to connect with others, it further reinforces the very hierarchy and boundaries we are working to dismantle.

Everyone can give and everyone can receive. No person on the receiving end of a gift wants to feel like they are receiving a gift out of pity. This steals the joy of the exchange for both giver and receiver.

All these considerations add up to a lot of pitfalls that would seem to go a long way to prevent us from engaging in acts of genuine giving other than the accidental encounter, such as my experience in the bread aisle. This may be why many religions have taken the brilliant step of institutionalizing the practice of giving—especially of giving money—in the form of guidelines, even commandments, which help us overcome our natural inertia and fear of giving.

Of course, this institutionalization is one way that groups within religion can raise money, and we will consider other parts of the following practices in later chapters, but for now, notice how each of the following traditions acts as a way of encouraging its followers to give not haphazardly, but intentionally and regularly, as an act of worship.

In the Christian tradition, the concept of the tithe is most often used to guide giving. Basically, a tithe is considered to be 10 percent of your income, and is based on text from the Hebrew Bible. In Deuteronomy 12 and 14:22–23, the Israelites are to give a tenth of their produce to support the temple, community, religious leaders, or those in need. In 2 Chronicles 31, King Hezekiah tells the people of Israel to give as a part of worship. In Genesis 28:10–22, Jacob promises to God a tithe of all he has. In Deuteronomy 26, the tithe is the first fruits of the harvest. Tithing is not required of Christians, but it is strongly encouraged.

In the Jewish tradition, giving charity is manifested in the concept of *tzedakah* (righteous giving). Jewish people believe that through their giving of funds to the synagogue or to the needy, they are offering reverence to God. They hold God in the highest regard by showing devotion through giving.

In Islam, *zakat* (2.5 percent of wealth given each year) is collected, typically during Ramadan, and distributed to the poor. *Sadaqah* (voluntary charity over and above *zakat*) is also collected by Muslims. In Islam, transferring a portion of your wealth to those in need is primarily an act of honoring God. Muslims are doing as they have been instructed by God when they give, so this act of devotion is worship.

In all these traditions, with their variances and idiosyncrasies, worshipers imitate God by reciprocating God's generosity, and show God devotion by embodying the command to give. (Jews and Christians use the phrase *imitatio Dei,* "imitate God," while Muslims use the phrase *takhallaqu bi-akhlaq allah*, "take on the qualities of God.")

Take a moment to consider the following questions, which are designed to help refine your thoughts and feelings about giving within your faith community.

- How does your faith community collect money?
- Is there an expectation from your faith community about how much money you should give? Does this affect your level of giving?
- Does giving money to your faith community feel any different than giving money to a secular nonprofit?
- When you give money to your faith community, does it feel like an act of worship for you?
- Would you describe God as generous? Why or why not?
- Do you feel closer to the Sacred when you give to another person?

How Money Is Collected

The logistics of giving often reveal a tradition's fundamental attitude toward giving money, and a thoughtful engagement of these practices can enhance your own experience of giving.

For example, a church in Augusta, Georgia, has installed "giving kiosks" (read: ATMs) in the narthex of the church. What does it say that there is a machine taking monetary donations just inside the church entrance? "Show me the money"? Perhaps.

On the other hand, some might say an ATM communicates that the organization wants you to have every opportunity to participate in every element of worship, including the offering. Whatever you think, there is a lot of meaning at stake in these details. Each choice a faith community makes as to how the collecting of money is handled affects how you will understand God, money, and their intermingling.

In Christianity, giving is frequently incorporated into a communal worship service; typically, a plate or basket is passed from one person to the other, throughout the congregation, and then is brought to the altar and offered as an act of devotion. The collection of the money is seen as a worship element just as prayer, the singing of hymns, and the readings of scripture are elements of worship. Where this act falls within the order of the service can lead to different meanings. If it falls at the beginning, somewhere around the announcements, the message could be that the collection of money is technical and just something that has to occur before the real meaningful elements can begin. If the collection comes after the centerpiece of the service—perhaps the sermon— it could be understood as a response to what parishioners have heard in the morning message. (I have heard of a church where a wealthy congregant routinely put a $1,000 check in the offering plate if she agreed with the pastor's sermon. If she didn't like what he said, she gave nothing.)

Renowned preacher Peter Gomes wrote, "White people who visit black churches are often surprised and not a little shocked at the number of offerings given, and with the fine art of encouraging people to generosity. It takes them some time to realize that the giving of money … is the central drama in the act of worship."[3]

Conversely, in many religious and spiritual communities, money is never handled at all during a worship service. In Judaism, for example, traditionally money is not to be carried, exchanged or collected on the Sabbath. Instead, money for suport of the synagogue is paid as membership dues and other fees (such as for High Holy Day service seating). *Tzedakah* (righteous giving), is often collected in the *pushke* (box to collect money) typically found in homes, synagogues, and schools. *Tzedakah* (righteous giving) is also a part of Jewish holidays, festivals, and life cycle events.

A system of local federations and Jewish philanthropies, as well as an increasing number of private foundations, also receive Jewish giving. That money is not actually collected during a service says to some, "Giving is not an act of worship." To others it says, "Giving is between you and God." The point is, how money is handled in a faith community matters, and we can narrate the choices made to convey a particular meaning.

Logistically, how is money collected in your tradition? Theologically, what does this say about money, God, and giving? Consider, for example, the rising trend of letting congregants make contributions electronically. Is automatically withdrawing money on a regular schedule a good idea when it comes to religious giving? Supporters of this approach point to convenience and reliability. When a family is away on vacation one Sunday, their bank is still withdrawing money and depositing it in the church's account. A misplaced bill for membership dues at the synagogue won't matter if the congregation has a credit card on file. Detractors argue that electronic giving misses the all-important ritualistic element present in traditional giving. It's the same problem as when we write a check to our faith community—or any other organization to which we give—on a quarterly or yearly basis. If my giving happens automatically or infrequently, I miss out on the opportunity to regularly remind myself of the abundance of God and the call to give out of that generosity. I am not embodying the act of generosity with any regularity and am missing the chance to train my mind (and body) to give. Instead, giving money becomes a mindless act that happens *to* me rather than an embodied act that I make happen. But when I regularly and deliberately give my money, I consciously reaffirm life as an abundant gift and turn my back on the cultural narratives that tell me accumulation is the only path to fulfillment.

WORSHIP OF MONEY

Besides giving money *as* worship and giving money *in* worship, there is, of course, the worship *of* money that is worth mentioning. It has been aptly observed that many people—even whole societies, you might argue—see money not as a means for worshiping God, but rather as the object of worship itself. My dictionary offers one definition of worship as "extravagant respect or admiration or devotion to an object of esteem" and even has "worship of the dollar" as an example.[4]

Many people wouldn't likely admit, or even be aware, that they worship money. But don't underestimate the seductive power of cash. In fact, money can impersonate God. Consider the following characteristics of money as described by Mark Vincent, a leader in issues of money and the church: "It outlives you.... Its circle of influence is greater.... It is mysterious."[5]

Even the feelings associated with worshiping money are similar to those associated with worshiping God: when you have money, you feel grateful and full of a certain type of joy. And each has similar effects in life: both money and God transcend all particularities of humanity (race, gender, class, sexual orientation) and become, as Georg Simmel wrote in his early twentieth-century work *The Philosophy of Money,* "the centre in which the most opposed, the most estranged, and the most distant things find their common denominator and come into contact with one another."[6]

It's little wonder that many fall into the trap of worshiping—to use a telling phrase—the Almighty Dollar. But the gratitude and joy you feel by having money are very different than the joyful gratitude you experience when you give money away. One is founded on your ability to amass and hold onto wealth, which for almost everybody is a never-ending battle you struggle to control. The other is founded on something always available to you, always within your power—taking the money you do have and giving it away. The paradox that we've explored is that when you give money away, you discover that the source of joyful gratitude isn't the money itself, but the transformation of heart and perspective that the act of giving achieves.

OTHER TYPES OF GIVING AS WORSHIP

Giving money may be a potent form of worship because of money's inherent power, but other forms of giving can also be acts of worship if they are undertaken in the same spirit of intentional reverence for God and involve feelings of joyful gratitude.

My husband is a Methodist pastor and we live in a parsonage owned by the local church he serves. Before we moved into the house we asked if we could replace some dated linoleum flooring with tile. Given the limited budget of the small church, we offered to donate the supplies and give our labor to do the project ourselves, with the help of my little brother who does tile work professionally. We had a fantastic week, and the three of us derived so much joyful gratitude from giving something to the church that they could otherwise not have afforded. It was a small, but significant, act of worship.

But like any form of giving, the week was not picture perfect. A soundtrack did not play in the background when I turned the water to the house back on and, unbeknownst to me, uncapped bathroom pipes drenched the walls. I was not smiling when I stepped right through the adhesive I had just spent thirty minutes perfectly spreading on the backer joints. And joy is not the emotion that comes to mind when I remember one parishioner's comment: "I really liked the linoleum."

No, this exchange of giving, like all others, was messy. But it was also fulfilling because of the connections I strengthened with my husband and brother, and the connections we made with our new parishioners. But even that wasn't perfect! After over fifty hours of working on that floor, every part of my body ached. And the reaction of our new parishioners to the new floor, which we had toiled so hard to create? "Looks good."

Looks good? Maybe I've watched too many home makeover shows and my expectations were too high. I wanted, "Astonishing!" I wanted, "Fantastic, absolutely unbelievable!" I wanted some tears. Instead, what I got was, "Looks good." But, really, that was enough. The real reward was the satisfaction in the act of giving itself and the relationships made and strengthened.

BE CREATIVE!

Worship can include *any* intentional act that offers reverence to God, no matter how grandiose or unassuming. That's exciting because it means you don't have to start a practice of giving with superhuman effort or enough money to bankroll a small company. Instead, you can begin right where you are and look to what makes you passionate for ideas on how to give as an act of worship.

For example, I happen to be passionate about the environment, both because my own religious tradition tells me that I should be a good steward of the earth (Genesis 1:28, 2:15) and because I just love clean air and a clean planet. When I moved to a new city just before getting married, I had an entire living room full of packing and shipping materials thanks to the move and to the large number of wedding gifts my husband and I received in the mail. Every inch of our living space was covered, wall-to-wall and floor-to-ceiling, with cardboard boxes, gift boxes, packing peanuts, ribbon, packing paper, and bubble wrap. I am proudly the poster child for Obsessively Organized Neat Freaks, color coordinating my closet on a weekly basis. Needless to say, this mess drove me crazy. I just wanted to use the wheelbarrow and haul it all out to the curb so the garbage collectors would take it all away ASAP. But I couldn't bear to see all this stuff not recycled or reused. So, taking this stuff to the garbage dump where it would pollute the earth just didn't work for me.

Instead, I viewed this as an opportunity to turn a normal, everyday activity into an act of worship. My husband and I began sorting the materials and finding uses for everything. We flattened all the cardboard boxes, loaded them from seat to roof in both of our cars, and drove them to a recycle yard that we found on the Internet. We took the bubble wrap to a local non-profit that helps grieving young people; they let the kids pop the bubble wrap as a way to let out their aggression. We took the packing peanuts to a mailing store that would reuse them, and sent over one hundred gift boxes to two organizations who had adopted families during the holidays and needed to wrap dozens of gifts. At times I wondered if it was really worth all this effort just to make sure materials did not end up in a landfill. But when I reminded myself that this act of giving was an act of worship—I was taking care of God's creation and imitating the Creator—it gave all that tedious work powerful meaning.

Rather than being an annoying series of errands, this work became an opportunity to worship. I felt connection to the earth as I dropped our heavy loads of cardboard onto mounting piles of recyclable material that I knew were being rescued from the alternative plight of taking up space in a landfill. I felt useful to a group of people I normally have no connection with as I offered material that children would use to deal with their loss of a loved one. I felt joyful gratitude knowing I was contributing to sustaining the earth.

Caring for the planet, advocating for the poor, befriending the elderly, giving love to a homeless animal—each one of us can worship God through creative and generous giving of our time, talent, and treasure. Look to the issues you are most passionate about for a place to begin your own practice. Here are just a few examples of how you can give nonfinancially in a way that would be worship:

Care for the environment. Take reusable bags with you when you go to the grocery store to avoid plastic bags, which are hard to recycle or reuse. Reusable bags also work great for trips to the big-box discount stores or even the mall.

Recognize all of humanity. As we are all children of God, take time to look the passing stranger in the eye. When you sit down in an airplane, acknowledge the person beside you with a hello. Give the gift of presence and recognition to a stranger.

Offer love to a homeless animal. Thirty minutes of your time can make a world of difference to an animal that is confined to a cage. If you have kids, the local humane society is a great place to spend a dull Saturday afternoon and the experience provides them with a powerful way to give.

Share your possessions. Are you getting married soon, or have you recently tied the knot? Consider donating your wedding dress to an organization that can either pass it on to a woman who could not otherwise afford a dress or sell it to raise money for a charitable cause.

Forgive and be patient with others. Whom do you harbor anger toward? Give them and yourself the gift of forgiveness. On a more casual basis, when someone makes a mistake or is just driving you crazy, be generous with your patience. By doing so, we imitate the nature of God.

Provide hospitality. Invite the spouse of an active military man or woman for dinner. On Mother's Day, welcome into your home a mother who has lost a child.

Care for our children. If we believe in God as creator, then we are all an extension of God's family. Spend time reading to children at schools. Attend a school play or band concert. Be a mentor or active role model. Adopt a child or be a foster parent.

Support the support staffs. Thousands of people spend each day "serving" others for a living. Give back to folks in the service industry. Throw away your trash after the movies and put the armrest back up. Return your shopping cart to the stall in the parking lot. Put away your food and tray at the café. You can even strip the sheets of your hotel bed and pile the bathroom towels; you'll really make the housekeepers' day.

Even these nonfinancial ways of giving should be carefully considered before making large commitments of time and resources. I have a friend who, after hearing a moving sermon about volunteering with the homeless, said of the pastor, "He makes working with the poor sound so poetic!" My friend signed up to volunteer one night a week and one weekend a month, expecting his "sacrifice" of time to be met with nothing but gratitude and enthusiastic thank-yous from the people he was helping. After six months he'd had enough of the reality of his work—which did not measure up to his expectations, as you might have guessed—and quit. It was an unfortunate loss for both him and the people he was serving and was a result of his naive expectations. There was joy to be found in his volunteer work, it just didn't look like he thought it would. He had to look deeper to find it in the connections he was making with other people, right in the midst of the challenges and conflicts he experienced.

LIVING THE GIFT

Giving as worship is just one component in the larger scheme of living a lifestyle of generosity. Next, we will consider giving as stewardship, which is essentially about living out another bit of good news: the Creator has provided us with an abundant amount of resources.

GIVING AS STEWARDSHIP

Managing Our Abundance

stewardship—*the conducting, supervising, or managing of something; especially: the careful and responsible management of something entrusted to one's care*
—Merriam-Webster Online Dictionary, www.m-w.com

Stewardship is a profound and often misunderstood concept. Its essential meaning is to assume the responsibility of managing resources—such as money, possessions, or land—that belong to someone else for the benefit of a third party. It is a concept that involves supreme competency and self-control: by definition, the steward wields great power over the resources and could mismanage the resources into ruin, or use them to benefit him- or herself. On the other hand, the steward could take advantage of the great gift and do something life-changing with it.

Unfortunately, the word *stewardship* has lost some potency in our modern usage, particularly in religious settings where it is often little more than a buzzword used in fund-raising campaigns to conjure up some kind of loose correlation between God and the giving of money. Countless desperate pleas for financial pledges have been uttered in the name of stewardship by distressed clergy who are worried that the organization's electricity might get cut off if the offering is low. The motive may be honest and direct, but the superficial use of such a profound concept both associates stewardship with feelings of guilt and fear and robs us of the opportunity to view the stewardship of our finances in a larger context—one that can transform some fundamental perceptions of our lives. Stewardship is about wise management, not fund-raising.

Indeed, stewardship is a responsibility—for the careful use of time, talent, and treasure—that we ignore at our own peril, for the natural consequences of ignoring this responsibility include pollution and poverty. At the same time, however, stewardship also provides us with a unique opportunity to discover the freedom we can experience when we stop clinging to the illusion that we actually "own" anything. When we realize that our possessions are merely on loan, as it were, we discover a light-heartedness and ease when dealing with money and objects that we may not have previously known. Indeed, practicing stewardship can be a lot of fun!

Scriptural Foundations for Stewardship

The concept of stewardship is nothing new. Foundational Jewish and Christian texts affirm that God, by virtue of creating the world in the first place ("In the beginning God created the heavens and the earth," Genesis 1:1), owns the world and everything in it. As the creator, God then entrusted humans as stewards of creation. In Genesis 1:28, the creation story continues: "God blessed (humankind), and God said to them, 'Be fruitful and multiply, and fill the earth and subdue it; and have dominion over the fish of the sea and over the birds of the air and over every living thing that moves upon the earth.'" We as humans are trustees of all that God owns (1 Peter 4:10).

This concept plays out in a variety of religious practices. In Judaism, the practice of *tzedakah* (righteous giving) is sometimes thought of as participation with God in the distribution of income to the poor, partnering in the divine process of sustaining life.

When money is given to a *tzedakah* (righteous giving) fund, it is seen as God's money, and those in charge of the fund get the chance to partner with God in putting those funds to use. The tithe is also referred to within the Jewish tradition, known more often as *ma'aser* (the Hebrew word for tithing). Jews are encouraged to give between one-tenth and one-fifth of their net worth and income. (But not more than that, as then you would be in need of *tzedakah* yourself.) You can find *ma'aser* calculators online that direct you through the maze of determining an appropriate amount to give. Jewish people will often set up a *ma'aser kesofim* fund in which they separate a tenth of their income to use for charitable purposes. By setting up a separate fund, you remind yourself that this money is not yours. This money belongs to God, and your role is to act as a trustee. In Jewish scripture, Rabbi Eleazar of Bartota reminds us, "Give (God) what is (God's), for you and yours are (God's)" (Talmud *Mishnah Abot* 3:7).

In Christianity, many adherents strive to tithe (give 10 percent of their income) directly to their local church, while recognizing that the remaining 90 percent they retain ultimately belongs to God and should be used responsibly. Liturgy, prayers, and songs during communal worship reflect this theory of stewardship. Consider some of the words in the Lord's Prayer, recited every week in many Christian congregations: "Give us this day our daily bread" (Matthew 6:11). These words ask God to provide for our circadian, materialistic needs. In other words, "What we have comes from You, God, so please keep it coming." Or consider the words of the hymn "We Give Thee but Thine Own," written in 1864 and still sung regularly today:[1]

> We give Thee but Thine own,
> Whate'er the gift may be;
> All that we have is Thine alone,
> A trust, O Lord, from Thee.

> May we Thy bounties thus,
> As stewards true receive;
> And gladly, as Thou blessest us,
> To Thee our firstfruits give.

These lyrics emphasize that all we have is from God, and from this bounty we can act as stewards and practice giving. Many children in the Christian church grow up knowing about the tithe from a very early age, including me. Tithing envelopes were mailed to our home each month, preprinted with our name and address. All we had to do was put in the money and indicate to which fund we wanted to contribute (general, organ, building, missions, or pretty much anything else that needed money to survive). Each Sunday morning, without fail, an offering envelope appeared on the kitchen counter in my house to be picked up on our way out the door to church. If we were absent one Sunday, the next Sunday would be a "two-envelope Sunday." (Mom and Dad let my brother and me put the envelope in the offering plate during worship, but they made it very clear you put it face down as an act of humility since the amount of the check was written on the front of the envelope.) To my knowledge, during the seventeen years I lived at home, our family never missed a Sunday of tithing. This consistent example is clearly one reason that my brother and I find it second nature to practice giving. It was just how things were for our entire childhood.

Islam also affirms that God, not we, owns everything ("Never let those who hoard the wealth which God has bestowed on them out of His bounty think it good for them," Qur'an *Al-Imran* 3:180) and has institutionalized stewardship practices. *Zakat* (alms tax) and *sadaqah* (voluntary charity) are practices of giving back a portion of God's bounty as stewards. God is seen as *al-Wahhab* (Ultimate Giver) and *al-Razzaq* (Ultimate Provider), and Muslims are granted ownership as trustees of God's creation.

Devout Muslims take calculating very seriously, using a questionnaire similar to an American tax form, and paying *zakat* (alms tax) each year, as it is an annual reminder of God's sovereignty and our role to act as steward. The process of calculating *zakat* invites you to acknowledge all of your wealth, from the amount of cash in your bank account to the amount of livestock you own. In other words, everything belongs to God.

On some level, it might be easy to blithely agree with the assertion of these three faiths that everything belongs to God and go about your life as normal. But I remember that the notion of God as the ultimate owner of my money and possessions finally sunk in when I was a child. I was, shall we say, just a *little* disappointed. I've always preferred to buy, not lease. I like to lead, not follow. And I definitely like having complete command over my stuff. In grade school I had a box of sixty-four Crayola crayons. It drove me crazy when kids would borrow them because, inevitably, they would blunt the sharp point of the crayon, put them back in the wrong color order, or, heaven forbid, break one. Truth be told, it took me at least a month after I got the box to actually use one of the crayons because I wanted to keep them perfect for as long as possible. That's how much I valued the little bit of control I had over those sixty-four uniquely colored objects; they were *mine*.

When I eventually came around to the idea that my crayon box was not really mine in the first place but was rather on loan to me for a while, I discovered a surprising sense of freedom—of relief, almost. I was freed from fretting over the inevitable demise of each perfectly sharpened crayon tip. I still had a momentary anxiety attack when I heard snap and saw a classmate with a piece of crayon in either hand. But I released the worry in my heart about messing them up and was freed simply to enjoy what had been loaned to me and to share it with others.

When you are able to see every component of your life—your money, your home, your car, your bank account—in this way, you find that you worry less and that giving generously is no longer threatening or a chore. Instead it becomes a life-enriching experience that underscores the abundance of what you do have. The secret is learning to hold your possessions more loosely. It's a strange paradox, but it's true: when you loosen your grip of control on your stuff, you find that you actually appreciate it more than you did when you clutched it for dear life. You also discover a freedom with (and from) your possessions that leads to joy in the act of giving.

TOWARD FREEDOM AND CREATIVITY

When giving is viewed as stewardship, you're able to let go of the trappings associated with possessing things and to expand your imagination to consider the possible uses for your sacred abundance.

I remember one Halloween when I was visiting a friend out of town and he needed to be gone for a few hours that evening. Those few hours were the prime trick-or-treating hours, so I offered to stay home and hand out candy at his house. He left me a big bowl of treats, and I had so much fun handing out that candy to the kids that came by. "Sure, take a couple. Heck, take three or four … it's not my candy!" I had this absurd sense of freedom because I was handing out someone else's stuff. Acting on someone else's behalf, with their resources, for the benefit of another—it was a delight. (By the way, this friend later became my husband.)

But what about when it's not candy, but cash? One of Oprah Winfrey's best-loved episodes is her annual "Favorite Things" show, where she spotlights her favorite (and often expensive) holiday gifts, and then lavishes each member of the audience with those gifts. On October 3, 2006, however, Oprah replaced that episode with one called, "Oprah's Favorite Giveaway Ever," in which she gave each member of her audience one thousand dollars—to spend on a *total stranger* in just one week.

Audience members seemed a bit confused at first—spend it on somebody *else*? But before long a sense of excitement washed over their faces at the invitation and freedom they'd been given. The money wasn't theirs to begin with, so the typical reservations and objections that come with giving away money did not apply. They weren't losing anything by giving it away.

This is the very model of stewardship that I am describing. By using someone else's money to help someone besides yourself, you can approach the task with a certain healthy detachment. The emotional energy usually reserved for fret and worry can instead be transformed into curiosity and a certain creativity—"Hey, let's try *this*! What do we have to lose?"

That's what happened with Oprah's audience. They had been given an opportunity to be creative, and all they really had to do was enjoy using the money to help someone else. The results of the "pass it on" experience aired two months later on the episode, "Oprah's Favorite Giveaway Ever: The Results." One participant paid it forward by buying plane tickets for parents of sick children to visit their kids in the hospital; the airline donated an additional forty tickets on the spot. Another audience member from a small town of fourteen thousand people decided to give her $1,000 to a dad with a brain tumor who has a family of nine children to support. With a few phone calls and an ad in the local newspaper, town locals added to her gift and raised $72,000. A first-grade teacher from Pittsburg returned home and decided to use her $1,000 to buy new shoes for the kids in her school. They enlisted the help of local shoe stores and the townspeople to raise $63,000 for the elementary school. Two Atlanta sisters turned $2,000 into $200,000 for a battered women and children's shelter. These audience members were not only creative in how they chose to gift their money, many were uninhibited by the limitations that typically accompany giving money. Instead, their philanthropic energy caught fire and multiplied the initial gift (and experience) exponentially.

You can experience this same freedom and creativity that the practice of stewardship brings, and you don't have to wait for a windfall or get lucky on the Oprah show. You just have to plan and learn to see your money (and other resources) as a steward would—to be used for others. This new way of thinking involves some unique challenges and even temptations, which we will explore, but the rewards are a transformed mindset as you experience life more abundantly than ever before.

It's worth noting that my own religious tradition conceives of stewardship as a command from God. So, for me, acting as a steward of the resources at my disposal is also an act of obedience to divine will. But you don't have to share my personal conviction to benefit from adopting a stewardship approach to life. Andrew Carnegie, for example, was a nonreligious philanthropist who based his idea of stewardship on a secular gospel of wealth. He believed that people of wealth were responsible for acting as trustees of the needy and were obliged to redistribute their assets. He once wrote, "Surplus wealth is a sacred trust which its possessor is bound to administer in his lifetime for the good of the community."[2]

Whatever spiritual path you follow, or even if you follow none at all, a moment's reflection will remind you that however much material wealth you amass in this lifetime, you leave it all behind the moment you die. In Islam, practicing *zakat* (alms tax) is a way to purify material possessions. In Christianity we are told, "But store up for yourselves treasures in heaven, where neither moth nor rust consumes and where thieves do not break in and steal" (Matthew 6:20). There is profound wisdom in the old saying, "You can't take it with you." Our possessions are fleeting at best, and clinging to them more desperately won't change that fundamental fact. If you instead choose to view your possessions as resources to be used for the benefit others, you will discover the freedom of true stewardship.

ABUNDANCE VS. SCARCITY: TWO WAYS OF SEEING THE SAME THING

It's a fact of life that two people can see the same set of circumstances and, based on their perceptions, preferences, and predispositions, draw two drastically different conclusions about the nature of the situation. For example, two people walking together down the same busy city street might have very different experiences. One whose mind is filled with worry may see danger lurking around every corner and threats emanating from every stranger passing him by. But his friend walking alongside, whose mind is serene, may see buildings whose architecture is a marvel of engineering and a wonderfully eclectic mix of humanity sharing the same sidewalk.

I happen to be more like the first person, the one whose mind is full of worry. I can see the potential for catastrophe in every situation. In fact, my husband hates it when I watch the nightly news because I come away an anxious ball of nerves. The bird flu is coming and we need to build a bunker; the neighbor might be a serial killer so don't talk to him; who knows what products in our house may be under recall so let's systematically search the Internet about each and every one. Similarly, it's easy for me to look at our financial picture and see the holes—What if we have an unexpected medical expense? How are we going to afford a college education for our children—who aren't even in utero? Will we have enough when it comes time to retire?

It's not surprising that this kind of mindset is a challenge to living a life of stewardship. The nagging belief that "I don't have enough" is a symptom of seeing the world as a place of scarcity. A mind that sees the world as a place of scarcity thinks there is not now, and never will be, enough to go around—not enough money, not enough food, not enough love, not enough anything. The natural response of a mind that sees scarcity is to grab for as much as it can get—for itself. It does not see resources as opportunities to help others, and it certainly is not a generous giver.

But we are all capable of another kind of mind, one focused on the goodness around us. This is the mindset I was in when I passed out that Halloween candy. Instead of worrying about the dwindling bowl of candy, I felt freedom giving out handfuls of sweets to each child. I could have worked out a matrix of scarcity, figuring so many trick-or-treaters coming per hour, times the number of hours left in the evening, divided by how many snacks were left in the bowl ... but that would have been a massive joy killer. Instead, I chose to trust that my friend had purchased enough candy and so felt that I had an abundance of treats for the kids. Feeling that I had enough already—indeed that I had extra-abundance—relieved my anxiety and gave me a sense of joyous freedom. A great Punjabi proverb says, "When a sparrow sips in a river, the water doesn't recede. Giving charity does not deplete wealth."

The same is true when it comes to our possessions: our frame of mind makes a big difference in what we see and believe. We can think that we don't have enough and we'll never have enough (and certainly not enough to give anything away); or we can realize that our lives already contain an abundance of money and other resources that we can freely give away because it was never really ours to begin with. In my own life, when I choose to see my money, my belongings, my time as not my own but given to me by God, I learn to let go of my worried thoughts and instead view the world through the lens of abundance. Because everything I have is a gift, I trust that I do already have an abundance, indeed an extra-abundance, and that I will always have enough. It is a way of seeing the world as a place of abundance, not scarcity.

Admittedly, this is a tough idea to conceive of when at this very moment there are eighteen thousand children dying every day from hunger, while my freezer is full of food.[3] Does that mean God does not want these people to have adequate resources? Absolutely not. The gross discrepancy of resources is an indica-

Houston Public Library
Check Out Summary

Title: Giving, the sacred art : creating a lifes
tyle of
Call number: 205.677 W951
Item ID: 33477458543629
Date due: 5/15/2014,23:59

tion that society has not done a good job in redistributing the possessions over which God has given us stewardship. We haven't been good stewards because we have ignored the wealth of resources already at our disposal to help others. Consider this eye-opening children's activity to illustrate where the world's food and wealth are distributed. Say we divide twenty-five children into the following three groups: four kids represent the world's high-income people, six kids represent the world's middle-income people, and fifteen kids represent the world's low-income people. Now we'll pass out the amount of food that exists in each of these groups. (If you want to see this in action, try using pieces of popcorn to represent one piece of food.) The high-income group gets fifty pieces of food per individual, the middle-income group gets seven pieces of food per individual, and the low-income group gets one piece for every three people.[4]

We perceive the dire humanitarian situations throughout much of the world as that much more tragic when we view life as full of abundance—if only we as individuals, societies, and nations would be better stewards of the astonishing abundance that we control. Not only do we deprive our fellow humanity of these gifts, we also miss out on the opportunity of discovering the life-changing reality of giving.

Having a worry-filled mind, I understand how difficult it can be to trust that you (and we, as a nation) already have enough—an abundance, in fact. Learning to be content with what we have is hard, particularly because we struggle against powerful cultural narratives that tell us, "You need more." Not long ago I drove past a billboard for a luxury car dealership that announced, "A strong want is a justifiable need." Good advertising copy, maybe, but simply not true. And when our boundaries become blurred, we suffer in the long run, which is something we'll explore shortly. The way we passionately pursue more and more material goods reminds me of a gerbil who's locked in a cage and can't seem to find her way off the wheel. Those of us who struggle to find material contentment, probably all of us to some degree, are like that gerbil that keeps going and going with no end in sight. It's no wonder we don't notice the abundance God has already provided for us—we're too busy running faster and faster to obtain more.

But we can learn to jump off the wheel and find a more content and peaceful way to live. One of my favorite Christian scriptures is Matthew 6:25–34, in which Jesus says, "Therefore I tell you, do not worry about your life, what you will eat or what you will drink, or about your body, what you will wear." God will take care of all our needs, even when we decide to give away part of what we have. There's enough Halloween candy for the entire neighborhood—so much that we can give away handfuls at a time and still not run out. God has provided sufficiently for the needs of all God's children; how we steward those resources is up to us. Take a deep breath … exhale … and remind yourself of the abundant resources God has provided.

FINDING YOUR EXTRA-ABUNDANCE

Once you have reached some level of material satisfaction—contentment with the amount and type of things you have, your bank-account balance, the market value of your car—you are free to think about what to do with the resources you have over and above the level needed to maintain that lifestyle. I call this surplus your extra-abundance. Quantifying this extra-abundance can serve as a practical basis for your giving.

You don't have to be a millionaire to have extra-abundance. And ensuring that you have some extra-abundance to work with doesn't mean that you take a vow of poverty and give everything away except one outfit, a bar of soap, and a box of ramen noodles. The goal of identifying your extra-abundance is to intentionally acknowledge how much money and resources it takes to support whatever lifestyle you choose to live, make a conscious decision to maintain or change this level of lifestyle, then figure out how much you have left over to give away.

Consider that on some level, you have *some* extra, even if it's a single dollar, to give away, and that the power is not in the amount of money you give but rather in the amount of intention you put into the act of giving itself. Also keep in mind that money has a notorious tendency to seep out of our wallets in sneaky ways. The "maybe this time" lottery ticket, the candy bar snagged at the last minute in line at the grocery-store, the small purchase off the online auction site—you are not likely to be aware how quickly these small amounts add up to a surprising sum if you don't write down your spending habits. The simple act of writing down what you spend will almost certainly reveal areas where you can save money very simply by saying no to some of those small (or perhaps large!) purchases.

Use the following simple guidelines, along with the worksheets in the back of this book, to help determine what your extra-abundance is:

1. The first step is to determine the amount of money you earn in a year, including salary, investment income, and any other money that comes in. (See the worksheet in appendix A for assistance.) This may take a little thinking and effort, but it is time well spent.

2. The second step is to determine the amount of money going out in a year. This includes actual expenses as well as money earmarked for savings, retirement, a college fund, and so forth. (See the worksheet in appendix B for assistance.) Again, this is not a particularly easy or quick task, but taking your time to make an accurate assessment will bear fruit later. The large payments may be easy to remember—rent or mortgage, car payments, school loans, credit card debt. The

real benefit of writing down every expense is in the smaller expenses that truly add up. Do you have a soft spot for electronics? Are you a smoker? Do you pay someone to cut the grass? This dollar amount is how much money it takes to support the level of lifestyle you are currently living. Be realistic and reserve judgments on what you're listing, especially if you are brainstorming with a partner. There will be a time later to analyze what you see. The goal here is to simply capture all the things you spend money on in a year.

3. You now have two numbers: your expenses and your income. Subtract your expenses from your income to arrive at the difference. (See the worksheet in appendix C.)

What difference is left over? If your expenses are more than your income, you are living beyond your means. If this is the case, you are certainly not alone; much of America is in the red and living paycheck to paycheck. While this is not a book about personal finances or getting out of debt, this book does not exclude those of you who find yourselves spending more than you are earning. You probably have extra-abundance in other areas of your life, and there are plenty of nonmonetary ways to practice giving, which we will talk about later. Meanwhile, as you work to get your own finances in a more stable position, which is a holy act, consider setting a small goal of extra-abundance for yourself. It may be that you set aside a ten-dollar bill at the beginning of next year and then wait with anticipation to see how you can use that ten-dollar bill as a sacred steward. Remember, stewards come in all shapes and sizes.

If your expenses are less than your income, the difference is your extra-abundance. By taking the time to quantify this number and actually write it down on paper, you know what you can actually afford to give away. The actual giving then becomes a source of joy, and you will reap the spiritual benefits of giving without the voice of fear nagging, "But can we afford it?"

THE SACRED ACT OF BUDGETING

The exercise above is a good place to start as you begin to experiment with giving as a sacred art. But for an even more effective long-term strategy that will help you build giving into your entire lifestyle, consider creating a budget for your household that includes giving as one of its priorities.

One of the greatest decisions my husband and I made early on in our marriage was to make this type of budget. It wasn't particularly difficult to do, beyond the challenge of being consistent. For an entire year, we kept all our receipts and entered them into a simple spreadsheet on the computer, putting each purchase in a basic category (food, entertainment, car, and so on). At the end of the year we totaled the categories and were surprised at what we found. We saw exactly how we were spending our money. Despite our waxing poetic about how much we care about the needs of others, some of our fiscal decisions did not reflect what we thought were our convictions. I was particularly surprised that I had spent an entire month's salary on clothes in just one year! I was so embarrassed and disappointed in myself; I had no idea so much of our money was going to what I thought was some innocent retail therapy. Such a revelation about my true priorities came from a simple computer spreadsheet! On the other hand, I also was pleasantly surprised to discover through this document just how much my coupon clipping pays off at the grocery store. Coupon clipping has always been motivating for me, in part because I always think of it as free money. I had never really kept track of it before, though, so the spreadsheet allowed us to celebrate the five hundred dollars that was now part of our extra-abundance.

In light of what we discovered, good and bad, we then created a budget for the following year. We organized our budget in three basic columns (see the worksheet in appendix D): expected income, expected expenses (parsed out in basic categories), and extra-abundance (money that will be given away). I set a healthy limit on my handbag obsession in the new budget and we incorporated the increase in our extra-abundance fund thanks to the continued use of grocery coupons. Our budget ended up looking about like this: 100 percent in expected resources, 75 percent toward living expenses/savings and 25 percent to the extra-abundance fund.

This was the first time I felt as though I fully embraced a lifestyle committed to stewardship—taking a full inventory of my resources, calculating my annual expenses, budgeting responsibly for next year's expenses. This required a change in perspective for me, an intentional effort, but the result was that our spreadsheet of expenses and our budget for the coming year had become sacred documents—a map to guide us on the sacred path of giving. Entering receipts into the computer had become a holy act. The spreadsheet was more than a list of lines and numbers; it told a story about where my priorities were. Jim Wallis, founder and editor of *Sojourners* magazine, says, "Budgets are moral documents. They clearly reveal the priorities of a family, church, organization, city, a state, or a nation [they show] us what we most care about."[5]

INCREASING YOUR EXTRA-ABUNDANCE

As a holy document, a budget is more than a snapshot of your financial situation. It can be an effective tool for managing your giving, but it can also help you find ways to increase your giving.

Generally, your income will remain relatively fixed, unless you find favor with Publishers Clearing House or come into an inheritance from your long-lost billionaire uncle. That means if you want to increase your extra-abundance, you will need to find ways of reducing your expenses. This can be accomplished in some creative and surprising ways, and often without affecting your overall lifestyle in a major way. Here are some possibilities:

- On a separate sheet of paper, make a list of the major categories within your budget (for example: clothes, groceries, eating out, car, vacations, and electronics). Without referencing the budget, list these categories in order of importance to you. Don't make any judgments; just ask yourself where you would prefer to spend your money. Now look at your budget and see if those desires are reflected in what's actually happening with your money. Are you spending twice as much money on magazine subscriptions as you are on haircuts, but you'd much prefer a haircut over a magazine? If so, go cancel some subscriptions and free up some resources for your extra-abundance.

- Give up or simplify one basic element of your lifestyle for the sake of having additional extra-abundance to give away. For example, I visit my favorite coffee shop most weekday mornings for a cup of java. If I made my coffee at home two mornings a week, I'd save about six dollars a week. In the course of the year I would have three hundred dollars to give away.

- Pick a category and find a way to make it less expensive. For example, reduce your grocery bill by buying generic products over name brands. Or buy second-hand books rather than new ones. Swap the expensive, chic designer clothes for still-hip and well-made discount alternatives.

- Consider increasing your extra-abundance by 1 percent each year. If you gave away 2 percent of your earned income this year, why not shoot for 3 percent next year? Figure out what that difference means in real dollars and make a plan for where that money will come from. For example, let's say that last year I made $35,000 and gave away 2 percent ($700) to charity. This year, with the same salary, I plan to give away 3 percent ($1,050). This difference is $350, and with the help of my budget I can proactively decide where those dollars will come from. There's no need to buy a new dress for my friend's upcoming wedding; I have one in my closet I can wear ($100). I can get my parents to pick me up from the airport over the holidays and not rent a car ($150). And I'll finally cancel that credit card I never use with the big annual fee ($100). There's my 1 percent increase for the year.

- If you're a visual person and like to see immediate results, consider the jar method of budgeting. Use your budget as a roadmap to guide you to places where you could save a few dollars here or there. Intentionally avoid making a regular purchase and instead put the money in a jar marked "extra-abundance." That cash can then be used at your discretion for others. This exercise can work particularly well with kids.

While these suggestions may be helpful, there are no magic formulas to use or secret percentages to be calculated. Being a good steward of money is knowing where our money has gone in the past, deciding where we want our money to go in the future, and living a life of intentionality to make those dreams a reality. In the larger picture, creating a lifestyle of generosity is about being aware of how you are living, recognizing what is at stake in your lifestyle choices, and ultimately thinking about the needs of others with your extra-abundance.

MANAGING WITH VISION: WHAT TO DO WITH YOUR EXTRA-ABUNDANCE

Being a steward and figuring out what to do with your extra-abundance is not simple. Even Aristotle agrees: "To give away money is an easy matter and in any man's power. But to decide to whom to give it, and how large, and when, and for what purpose, is neither in every man's power nor an easy matter."

Bob Payton and Michael Moody, two scholars in the field of philanthropy, have this to say about our role in managing God's gifts with vision:

> Stewardship is about more than maintenance, it is about visionary management. Stewards have temporary control over, but not ownership of, an inheritance. They also have an obligation to manage this inheritance in such a way that it can be passed along even better and stronger than it was when they received it. There is a profound implication of trust in the idea of stewardship—"steward," "trustee," and "curator" are in many ways comparable terms.[6]

Payton and Moody make an excellent point about the idea of trust within the context of stewardship. A steward doesn't maintain an inheritance (in their example) haphazardly or recklessly; he or she acts responsibly and with purpose. I like to think about this in terms of having vision—both a purpose for what you want to achieve with your giving and the ability to discern when to give and when to set limits and boundaries.

Sometimes this means establishing limits on your own spending for yourself and others. I'll never forget Christmastime as a child. Each year my parents would determine how much money they wanted to spend on presents for my brother and me. Dad would give Mom that amount of money in an envelope. When the money in the envelope ran out, that was it. Mom had so much fun buying presents with her stash. She would write down how much she spent at each location, and keep a running total of how much she had left. Before they had set up this system, Mom was always angst-ridden about spending money on presents. "This skateboard costs fifty dollars ... that's a lot of money ... I've already bought Christian a pair of blue jeans and the drum kit ... maybe I should call Hugh and consult with him (again) on how much money he wants us to spend on the kids this year ... I just feel guilty spending more money." Mom loves to shop, but the fun had been sucked right out of Christmas shopping during those years. But when she and Dad planned ahead with some vision and placed clear limits on what they wanted to spend (even if they didn't know what, exactly, they would buy), shopping was no longer a dreaded, anxiety-producing experience. Any disagreement or worry about how much to spend was dealt with beforehand; a decision was made and the shopping commenced. Mom felt freedom buying the gifts and didn't feel guilty about spending the money.

At other times managing your money means putting limits on what others can expect from you; one of the perils of freely giving away your extra-abundance is to give it away *too* freely. It can be tempting to just go for it and give the money away randomly to whatever causes pop up, but it's okay to say no to people or organizations who ask for money. We probably all know someone like this—an extremely generous person who writes a check the minute a need is expressed, usually without thinking about whether she has the money to give or whether the source of the need is even legitimate. And most all of us have probably given impulsively at one time or another. The problem is a lack of vision and limits for how, where, and when you want to give, and the consequences could be that your extra-abundance runs out more quickly than you'd like, or worse—the cause that seemed so urgent in the moment may turn out to be less important to you than others that you *truly* want to help.

The fact is, you can't help everyone who deserves it. You probably can't even help everyone you want to help. But you can develop some basic guidelines that direct your giving to a more specific audience, thereby freeing yourself from the anxiety of second-guessing and wondering, "Should I have given to them, too?" In turn, these guidelines will help you refine your vision for giving. Stewardship is about proactively creating a structure for giving based on personal interests and the needs of the world, rather than allowing giving to be a reactionary act that happens based only on appeals.

DISCOVERING YOUR PERSONAL VISION FOR GIVING

Being a good steward is not just about *what* you give, it's about *how* you give. Having a vision will allow you to make the most of however much you're able to give away.

In his book *Strategic Giving,* philanthropy and public-policy scholar Peter Frumkin writes that donors in our modern society need to be more strategic in their giving in order for their gift to be used more effectively. "Although the amount of money given away each year continues to rise, there are lingering doubts about what the billions of dollars backed by good intentions have ultimately produced.... It remains difficult ... to see how the many small and isolated success stories of donors around the country ever amount to anything vaguely resembling a meaningful response to any of the major social problems ... that private philanthropy has long targeted."[7]

How do you achieve a vision for your giving? Begin by asking yourself a few simple questions. Is there a cause that you are particularly passionate about? What do you want to see changed about this world? Is there a particular group you feel is in need of support? If you are not sure what causes are most important to you, spread your philanthropic dollars across a few different causes. Getting involved in several causes is an excellent way to discover what you are most passionate about.

Here are some helpful hints to help determine your personal vision for giving:

- Think about your own personal history and the people or organizations that have been influential in your life—educational institutions, health care organizations, para-church groups, social service agencies. Make a list of specific groups that you might want to give money to as a way of saying thank you.
- What groups of people catch your focus most intensely? Sick children? Grieving teenagers? Alzheimer's patients? International orphans? Those suffering from mental illness? Consider focusing your giving around this particular group.
- If you were Superman and could give the world one thing, what would it be? A cure for cancer? World peace? The alleviation of AIDS? How might you (minus the Superman persona) be a part of making this dream a reality?
- What interests you most? Addressing systemic issues in order to prevent the problem? Give money to research. Assisting people with immediate needs such as education or counseling? Give money to direct service organizations. Educating the general public and influencing public policy? Give money to advocacy organizations. Keep in mind that an issue such as AIDS will have groups that are doing all of these things, and they are all good. But it's best to try and focus your dollars on one area.
- What legacy do you want to leave when you die? How does this influence where you give your extra-abundance?

A Word about Giving to Organizations

As you develop your vision for giving away your extra-abundance, one particular challenge is discerning precisely to whom you will give it. Whatever your passion, there is sure to be an organization you can give to that will happily accept your donations, but there are some important practical things to consider when determining how to give your money. Americans receive dozens of charitable solicitations for money in the mail each year, so the problem is not a lack of options for where to give. The problem is narrowing down all those pleas for money and determining who to help: Your local faith community? National disaster victims? A food bank? Wildlife preservation? There are 1.7 million nonprofits to choose from! Here are some guidelines to help you through the labyrinth of charities:

- Use the previous exercise to clearly identify those causes that you are most passionate about or are at least interested in. My husband and I, for example, are still discovering those causes and issues that move us the most, so we give to four basic groups: the arts, poverty, education, and our local church. Each year our giving focuses just a bit, but for now we cast a relatively wide net. Having said that, beware of spreading your philanthropic interest too thin, as you want to leverage your resources and get the biggest bang for your buck. Giving a few dollars here, a few dollars there, diminishes the impact of every dollar. Focus your giving as much as you are comfortable with.
- Once you have identified the cause(s) you want to support, identify specific organizations that are doing work in that area. If your interest is the environment, for instance, there are all kinds of groups you could support, from national groups that work for legislative change, to regional groups that organize recycling programs, to local groups that campaign to keep a particular river clean.
- You may already know of some specific organizations, but time spent researching other organizations is time

well spent; after all, 1.7 million organizations is a lot. Check out www.guidestar.org (registration is required but free), the flagship database for IRS-recognized U.S. nonprofits, to "verify a nonprofit's legitimacy, learn whether a contribution will be tax deductible, view a nonprofit's recent Forms 990, or find out more about its mission, programs, and finances." This is a great site to either learn more about an organization you are currently familiar with or discover new organizations doing work in your field of interest. Each type of organization has pros and cons, so it's just a matter of weighing all the options. A newer organization might be doing innovative things that revolutionize the field, but they also might burn out quickly and shut down. A multibranch, nationwide charity does take a lot of manpower to run, but the networking that can occur makes efficient use of every donated dollar.

• Donors frequently ask me for the red flags indicating that a charity is financially corrupt. My main piece of advice is this: it's to the organization's advantage to be as open and honest as it can be about financial matters. So, if you feel like a charity is being sneaky or not giving you the full story, trust your instincts. Also keep in mind when learning about organizations that overhead costs are to be expected. An organization needs funds for administration and fund-raising in order to exist. The Center on Philanthropy at Indiana University and the Center on Nonprofits and Philanthropy at the Urban Institute produced a donor's guide for nonprofit overhead costs. In it they suggest that "overemphasis on low overhead, far from enhancing the efficiency of charitable organizations, has reduced their effectiveness and corrupted their accounting."[8] So, when doing your research on your charity of choice, financial integrity is much more important than finding a charity that spent no money on fund-raising and is squeaking by with a computer running Windows 3.0. Look for overhead costs in the area of anywhere from 10 to 35 percent and only compare cost ratios of like charities.

- Once you select the organizations you want to support, consider *how* you want to support them. Charities can use your money most effectively when they know what to expect from you. The most efficient gift from a donor is money that comes in on a consistent basis, never takes a hiatus, and never decreases. Haphazard giving is, unfortunately, inefficient giving. Every time a solicitation letter is sent reminding you to send in your donation, the organization is paying for staff time and postage to produce that correspondence. Even if you're sending in ten dollars a year, you want to make the most of that ten dollars. So send it in regularly and faithfully.

- Along the same lines, give one larger amount of money rather than more frequent smaller amounts. Again, this cuts down on processing costs and time that the organization puts out with each donation they receive. It also avoids diluting the importance of your gift.

- Consider leaving a certain amount of funds reserved for emergency philanthropic situations. At least once a year a situation occurs where I really want to help but did not anticipate the need. Natural disasters, house fires, and terminal illnesses are all examples of reasons communities rally together and support one another. I like to set aside part of my extra-abundance funds so I can participate when these things happen. The key is to set up a system so you don't forget about your emergency fund.

- Remember, it's okay to say no. Wesley Willmer, former chairman of the Christian Stewardship Association, once wrote, "A modern-day fact of life is that you are bombarded with financial appeals from all sides—through the mail, at the office, on radio and television, via phone and e-mail.... The manner in which these appeals are made affect your spiritual formation, both consciously and unconsciously."[9] Despite all the thought and preparation you may put into where you will give your money to charity this year, at least a dozen other organizations will try to appeal to you for just a few more dollars. Don't undermine your philanthropic effectiveness by feeling pressured to give from your extra-abundance every time someone asks. Managing your resources effectively means sometimes saying no.

- Don't ever feel pressure to give money away quickly; you can always sleep on it. Pressure to give immediately may be a sign of a scam. A favorite saying of mine comes from an ancient Christian text, *Didache* 1:6 (Roberts-Donaldson Translation): "Let your alms sweat in your hands, until you know to whom you should give."

- Consider getting personally involved in the organizations you support financially. Whether it's volunteering in some capacity or just taking a site visit, your check will mean a lot more if you have some hands-on experience with where your money is going. My husband and I support an organization that helps grieving young people, but only recently did we actually get involved by volunteering over 250 hours chairing the organization's annual fund-raising gala. Hearing the stories from these kids firsthand about losing loved ones, and watching them tear up just at the thought of their family members, forever changed how I write my annual check. How might you get involved?

- Keep a detailed record of your giving throughout the year. This will be your best friend come tax time. Most gifts are tax deductible, but not all, so it's helpful to note this on your record. You'll save yourself an added step in March if you keep records now, along with a file containing all the letters from organizations thanking you for your donation and documenting your gift.

- Depending on how much money you are giving away each year, you might consider opening a separate bank account for charitable donations. Some people find it helpful to physically delineate funds so they're not tempted to spend their extra-abundance on themselves. This system can also be helpful for tax purposes because you have a clean record to deal with thanks to your bank statement.

- Avoid procrastinating. Writing checks at the tail end of December in hopes they will get postmarked within the calendar year is no fun, and charities are confronted with a surge of checks to process at the end of the year. Do everyone a favor and write those end-of-the-year checks or give online early in the month of December (if not sooner).

- Consider making one major gift within your lifetime. Over time, your philanthropic interests will become clear and you will most likely find one organization you identify with most. After the kids have gone to college and the house is paid off, dream about what kind of large donation might be possible. You can certainly do this giving via your will, but giving a gift to an organization while you're alive allows you to experience the joy of seeing your money put to use and being involved with the organization as it implements your gift.

Organizations, of course, aren't the only places our money can go. Every day we have the opportunity to help individuals and families directly. We will talk about this more in a later chapter, where we explore giving as a form of charity.

MONEY—SACRED OR PROFANE?

This is a good place to address a concern that commonly arises whenever I give seminars in a religious or spiritual context about having money, spending money, and giving money away. Inevitably, someone raises their hand and asks some variation on this question: "Isn't money the root of all evil? Should we really be talking so much about money, money, money?"

I understand the genuine concern behind the question, but I think the question is misguided. My first response is almost always to point out that, "Money is the root of all evil," is a tragic misquote of 1 Timothy 6:10, which actually reads, "The love of money is a root of all kinds of evil." In other words, as the writer of this Christian scripture wisely observes, money itself isn't a problem. It's our disordered understanding of money's proper, and even useful, role in our lives that is the genesis of trouble. The trouble isn't with material things, per se, but rather, "our difficulty is, as Wendell Berry puts it, our 'fundamentally ungenerous way of life,' our captivity to endless … acquisition."[10] We can so easily fall prey to the desire for more and more resources without any system for their use. Our cravings for money and possessions are dangerous because they focus on the money and possessions themselves, not on what those resources can accomplish for the greater good. Another way of putting it is to say that money itself is neither sacred nor profane—it's our own attitude and actions toward it that make it either a sacred or profane element in our lives.

A rightly ordered use of money and possessions means a valuing of them for their instrumental worth toward another end. That end, I would argue, is achieved by giving. Eighteenth-century theologian John Wesley was famous for saying: "Earn all you can ... save all you can ... give all you can." Stewardship not only encourages us to have a healthy view of money, it *requires* that we engage with money in a clear-eyed and wholehearted way.

While some might take issue with the idea of accumulating great amounts of wealth, I find it hard to argue with such a plan as long as the money is being acquired legally and ethically and is undertaken ultimately for the sake of helping others.

Yet, keep in mind that amassing a great fortune without focusing on the self is exceedingly difficult, so it should not be taken on lightly. Everything in our culture tells us to spend any extra we have on ourselves or possibly on our closest family and friends. For this reason, we must acknowledge that having wealth does bring with it unique responsibilities and worries of its own; remembering this fact can help us keep a giving perspective. Those who are stewards of large amounts of money and those who are stewards of small amounts have different issues to deal with, but both can lead holy lives. When the super-rich give a great deal of money away, they typically continue to retain a great deal. Even though their philanthropy may appear very generous when compared to others, they typically are not giving away a large percentage. Warren Buffett's $42 billion was particularly significant for that reason; it was virtually his entire wealth. But there are also plenty of examples of working-class individuals who have given away extraordinary percentages of their wealth. Albert Lexie, for example, has been shining shoes in Monessen, PA for over forty years at local businesses and the Children's Hospital of Pittsburgh, living on $10,000 a year. He has donated over $100,000 of his tips to the hospital, providing financial assistance to children who need treatment but cannot afford it.[11] Whether you give most of your money and possessions away and live among the poor or earn great amounts of money and leverage it for the sake of others, giving can be a sacred act. How are you using what you have (how ever much that is) for the benefit of others? How are you making a difference with your resources?

CREATIVE AND EFFICIENT USE OF NONMONETARY EXTRA-ABUNDANCE

Creating a lifestyle of generosity has as much to do with how we use our nonmonetary resources as it does with how we give away money. For example, do you have stuff sitting around in a basement or buried in a closet that you aren't using? Most of us do. As a proper steward of those goods, give them away to someone who can use them. Here are a few practical tips for being a good steward with your possessions:

- Go through your house the first Saturday of each month for ten minutes (set the kitchen timer) and collect at least three things you are not using that could be given away to someone else. Don't let things sit around and collect dust; let someone else have the privilege of their use. Giving away three things a month may sound like a lot, but, chances are, you're *purchasing* more than three new things a month. The goal is to purge your possessions on a regular basis rather than once every couple years or only when you move. Don't forget about the basement and attic, two very dangerous places—things get lost forever.

- Keep a permanent "give-away" box in your house. Whenever you come across something you no longer want or need, put it in the box immediately. Whenever you have five minutes, go through one drawer in the house and pull out any give-aways. When the box gets full, take it to a charity that can sell it in their thrift shop. Check out websites that specialize in posting used items available for free to members of the community. Getting rid of a little bit here and there will keep the clutter contained and will make sure you're storing only what you're actually using.

- One of the biggest enemies of stewardship is disorgani-
  zation and clutter. How many of us bought another pair
  of scissors, not because we don't have any, but because
  we can't find the ones we know we already own? When
  things are put away in boxes in inaccessible locations,
  you can bet you aren't going to use them. When we stay
  organized we don't buy unnecessary duplicates. In my
  house, for example, I have all my handbags hung on
  small hooks so I can see them. I used to keep them in
  boxes on high shelves. I ended up only using a few of
  them over and over and would purchase more because I
  wasn't aware of how many I already had. Now that I
  can see exactly what I have, I switch them out on a regular basis, and I'm less inclined to buy more because I
  have a visual image of what I already possess.
- When you go shopping, whether at the grocery store, a
  surplus warehouse, or the mall, make a list of what you
  need before you go. If something's not on the list, don't
  get it. You could allow yourself one unplanned item, to
  give yourself a little flexibility, but whatever you decide,
  make a plan and then stick to it.
- To avoid the accumulation of stuff, when you purchase a
  sweater (or other item of clothing), pick one sweater to
  give away. Not only does this keep your closet from
  becoming a mess, it provides an easy way to stay within the
  amount of resources you have committed to living with.
- When making a purchase, ask yourself the following
  questions:
    - Do I need it? If no, why do I want it?
    - Was the person who produced the product or
      service treated well?
    - How many hours of work will this cost me?
    - How often will I use it each week?

- Do I already have something similar that will serve the same purpose?
- How long will it last?
- Are the resources used to make it renewable?
- Could I borrow or rent it instead?
- Tomorrow morning when I wake up, will I be sorry I spent the money?
- Will anyone be disappointed I bought this?

- Take good care of the things you already own. Because we live in an age where mass production makes consumer goods cheap and easily obtainable, we tend to be careless with or hard on the things we own. Even though you may have the money to replace something, do your best to make it last as long as it can.
- Find ways to let others borrow items from you so they don't have to buy them. Not only can this save them money, but it can help you justify that big snowblower that only gets used a few times a year.
- Consider what will happen when you die. Don't let the government determine where your money and possessions will go. Prepare now to make a lasting difference. Create a will and consider planned giving. Less than half of American adults have a will, and only a small percentage have a charitable organization included in their will. By creating this document, you can have a say as a steward in where your resources go when you die.

You can also steward your time and talents—in other words, make good use out of the days and the abilities you have been given. Be a proactive, not a passive, steward. Here are some ways you can offer up the gift of your time:

- Provide hospitality by inviting others into your home to share a meal or even just to visit as a way to steward

both your home and your time—using them for the
benefit of others.

- See your daily errands as time to live out your identity as a steward. When you decide which stores to
shop at, for example, think about how they are treating their employees. Money is power, so when you
purchase from a particular company, you are giving
them your support. Just by making everyday purchases you can make a difference by supporting sustainable agriculture, small businesses, or living wages
for employees. Purchasing particular products can
also support social causes; our choice of a hybrid vehicle, for example, was a vote with our dollars for the
environment.

- Give to your local animal shelter or humane society.
Money is always a great gift, but animal shelters and
humane societies often have a wish list of items that
they need. The items they are looking for may range
from the inexpensive (cleaning supplies and pet treats)
to the expensive (computer software or computers). Call
your local shelter to find out exactly what they need
and tack the item onto your shopping list. When you
drop off the item, you can stop in for a while to pet the
cats or take the dogs for a walk. It will brighten the day
of an animal that may otherwise be confined to a cage,
and will brighten your day as well.

- Find out where your money is going when you invest
in companies through the stock market. Being socially
responsible with your investments is a relatively easy
way to participate in God's invitation to stewardship.
One rabbi wrote that we are "custodians of money for
the poor. We can take chances with our own funds, but
not those that belong to others."[12] Muslims are encouraged to invest their funds responsibly. For example,

money should not go toward pork, pornography, banks, alcohol, and other forbidden activities.

- What are you good at? Baking? Auto repair? Sewing? Gardening? Listening? We can't all sing like Pavarotti or paint like van Gogh, but we all can do something that can make a significant contribution. Whatever it is that you do well, that gift has been bestowed on you in abundance for the purpose of helping someone else. Keep your eyes open for ways you might be able to use your talent to help others. (Many faith communities keep informal databases of skills that their members possess, so it might be helpful to inform your lay leaders of how you can be of help.)

STEWARDS ARE PROACTIVE AND INTENTIONAL GIVERS

Practicing giving as a form of responsible stewardship involves work—there's no doubt about it. But it doesn't have to be a chore. When you realize the abundance already present in your life, you experience freedom from the clamoring craving for more, more, more. When you set clear and helpful limits on your spending, you experience the freedom that using your money wisely for the sake of others—as a steward does—can bring.

One of the primary reasons for taking the time to figure out your income and expenses is that it enables you to be proactive in your financial giving. It's about being mindful and aware rather than going through life with blinders on, only reacting to what comes along your path. If you figure out that you have one thousand dollars of extra-abundance each year, make giving a priority at the beginning of the year. Otherwise, that one thousand dollars will easily be subsumed into fast-food meals, blue jeans, electronic gadgets. Plan ahead so you're not giving from what's left over at the end of the year. Give from the top, not from the bottom where all the dregs settle. Giving is a spiritual discipline that requires commitment. Circumstances will always arise throughout the year and thwart your intentions to give—unless you have planned ahead. So, give away your first fruits to God, not the scraps (Proverbs 3:9).

Assessing your financial situation and making a plan is a holy act! Remember, spreadsheets can become sacred documents. God invites you to manage all that God has created, an invitation we should all be honored to accept. If you are systematic and strategic on the front end, you'll be free to enjoy the process of giving as you go. There's plenty of Halloween candy to go around, so enjoy every moment of giving it away.

GIVING AS
HOLY OBLIGATION

Transforming Identity through Discipline

obligation—*something one is bound to do*
—Merriam-Webster Online Dictionary, www.m-w.com

As a child I dreamed of becoming a renowned pianist who graced the stage of Carnegie Hall, the orchestra pit of Broadway, or the sanctuary of the Crystal Cathedral (my grandmother's favorite Sunday-morning program). My mom is an accomplished pianist, and I was said to have some modicum of musical talent myself, so I didn't think it would be so hard to become the pianist of my dreams. It would all just come very naturally, right? When my parents enrolled me in piano lessons in first grade, I relished the chance to finally get my hands on the keyboard.

I did not, however, feel such passion when it came to studying music theory. Who cared about scales, intervals, or inversions? Not this six-year-old. Why all this work? I just wanted to play like Liberace, minus the lavish wardrobe. But my mother, knowing what it took to become proficient on the instrument, made me do my theory homework week after week after blessed week. I did what she told me, but I certainly didn't understand why it was necessary.

Today, as an adult, I understand what my mother was doing: developing in me a discipline and routine that allowed me to slowly grow into the musician I am today, with professional theater and vocal credentials now on my resume. As a child I couldn't fathom the benefit of all that obligatory work. And it was *work*. Left to my own devices, I never would have done it. My mother, however, knowing I would never have progressed beyond playing "Chopsticks" had I not put the effort into my theory homework, obliged me to do it so that I could experience my best. Her loving nudge of parental authority provided me with the motivation I lacked, helped me overcome my natural reluctance, and enabled me to reap the benefits I could not see at the time.

Every religious tradition has at least a few practices that are obligatory—activities that its followers are told, even commanded, to follow. From the outside, such practices may appear to be rote or burdensome. Even from the inside, such obligations aren't always fun, and the benefits may not be readily apparent. But dig a little deeper and you are likely to find something more profound at work in these practices.

For some religious groups, giving is one of these obligatory practices, and wisely so, because giving—especially giving money—can be a difficult thing to do. We may be hampered by an excessive need for financial security or a tendency to acquire that may be a subtle form of greed. Or we may have an actual aversion to giving, perhaps because we see the recipients of the donations as undeserving or the organizations as bloated. Or we may simply be apathetic about giving, seeing it as just one more good idea of things we "should" do, like eating our vegetables and flossing.

But giving has the power to help us exchange our greed, aversion, and indifference for a compassionate perspective and a renewed engagement with the world. In short, it has the power to change our very identity into one of generosity.

But such changes take time, and progress toward that goal may not always be readily apparent. Sometimes it might seem like work, even a sacrifice, and often it is. But just like my mother obliged me to practice my scales, obliging yourself to give provides you with the motivation you may lack when the going gets tough, until you can see and experience for yourself the transformative joy of giving, first with your money and then with the rest of your life.

The ways in which different faiths emphasize obligatory giving can highlight how we can enrich our own experience of giving. Let's consider how three faiths—Judaism, Islam, and Christianity—exemplify this type of obligatory giving and what we might learn from each.

JEWISH *TZEDAKAH*—FORMATIONAL RIGHTEOUSNESS

My husband and I are big Broadway musical junkies, and one of my favorites is *Fiddler on the Roof.* There is an exchange in the show between beggar Reb Nahum and a man on the street that goes like this:

> Reb Nahum: "Alms for the poor, alms for the poor ... "
> Man: "Here, Reb Nahum, is one kopek."
> Reb Nahum: "One kopek? Last week you gave me two kopeks."
> Man: "I had a bad week."
> Reb Nahum: "So if you had a bad week, why should I suffer?"[1]

In Judaism, *tzedakah* (righteous giving) is a particular form of giving that is a *mitzvah*—a duty or obligation to fulfill the will of God. *Tzedakah* is so essential to Jewish identity that being a Jew means practicing *tzedakah*. To not give to those in need would mean to not behave in a Jewishly correct way.

But like other *mitzvot* (duty to God), the obligation is more nuanced than a mere "do this or else" commandment. It is an opportunity to devote yourself to God's purpose in the world. Specifically, *tzedakah* (righteous giving) is a moral obligation in which all Jews are commanded to help those in need through monetary, material, or other assistance so that everyone has the basic requirements necessary to sustain a dignified and decent life. No one is exempt from the practice of *tzedakah*. The Talmud says, "Even a poor man who himself survives on charity should give charity" (Talmud *Gittin* 7b), something the beggar Reb Nahum in *Fiddler on the Roof* may have conveniently forgotten. And refusing or neglecting to give is a serious matter: "If a person closes his eyes to avoid giving (any) charity, it is as if he committed idolatry" (Talmud *Ketubot* 68a).

Over time the emphasis of *tzedakah* has come to be focused on the giving of money, but it is actually intended to be broader in its scope. The word *tzedakah* itself literally means "righteous giving" and combines the concepts of charity and justice. Practicing *tzedakah* can be seen as a way of cultivating a new perspective and a new way of being in the world. Indeed, the obligation to contribute to the needy presents a powerful opportunity to transform our deeply rooted desire to *take* into a desire to *contribute*. As a rabbi colleague described to me, *tzedakah* is "our effort to tame and to channel the acquisitive instinct of the baser side of ourselves." It is an opportunity to reshape our identity. Obligatory actions lead to transformation of self.

Perhaps this is why the nineteenth-century Rabbi Israel Meir Kagan, better known as the Chafetz Chaim (the title of his first work) declares that those who oblige themselves to giving a certain amount of money receive greater benefit than those who give casually, even if the gifts are of equal value:

Those who adopt the practice of setting aside one-tenth or one-fifth of all their earnings, perform a greater deed

charity than those who give without assuming the obligation, even if the amounts in both cases turn out to be the
same. The latter fulfill the mitzvah [duty to God] of
tzedakah [righteous giving] only. The former, however,
form a partnership with heaven, and so their commercial
activities as such have the advantage of being a mitzvah.
This applies especially when, at the time of assuming the
... obligation, the person had in mind that God would be
sharing in all his undertakings.[2]

When we commit ourselves to obligatory giving we commit to
more than the act of donating money—we commit ourselves to a
mindset of generosity, to seeing the world in terms of, "How can I
help?" not, "What can I get?" We literally change the way we react
to the needs of others. Instead of responding with isolated moments
of benevolence, we commit to operating out of a greater framework
of active compassion that permeates every moment of our being.

ISLAMIC *ZAKAT*—AN IDENTITY TAX

Fundamental to Muslim belief and practice are the Five Pillars of
Islam, core teachings that every Muslim must subscribe to, such
as *sawn*, fasting during Ramadan, and *salah*, practicing prayer
five times daily. The third pillar of faith is an alms tax called
zakat. *Zakat* is a fundamental and obligatory requirement of faith
commanded by the Qur'an: "If they repent and take to prayer
and render the alms levy, they shall become your brothers in the
Faith" (Qur'an *Al-Tawbah* 9:11).

All Muslims who exceed a standard of eligible wealth called
nisab are required to give 2.5 percent of their net worth or wealth
(not income) away to the needy. This annual tax includes, for
example, levies on cash, savings and checking accounts, stocks and
mutual funds, and retirement plans. It does not include things that
are requirements of life such as a home or tools necessary for a
trade. Gold and silver jewelry are taxed, but precious stones in the

jewelry, such as pearls or diamonds, are generally not; jewelry is a much debated topic in *zakat* (alms tax) discussions. The exact percentage of the tax, ranging from 2.5 to 20 percent, depends on which category of wealth the item falls in—such as agricultural produce, items mined from the earth, livestock. A number of online *zakat* calculators are available to help navigate the maze of exemptions and various groupings and percentages.

Zakat has many nicknames—wealth tax, alms tax, poor tax—although it literally means "to grow in purity." In this, like *tzedakah* (righteous giving), *zakat* also has ties to personal righteousness. The Qur'an itself makes this explicit: "The righteous man is he who ... gives away his wealth to kinsfolk, to orphans, to the destitute, to the traveler in need and to beggars, and for the redemption of captives" (Qur'an *Al-Baqarah* 2:177). I like to think of *zakat* as an identity tax; when you give *zakat* you can allow that annual levy to make you a more generous person.

And yet the ramifications of *zakat* extend beyond the personal to the communal. The Prophet Muhammad said "He who sleeps on a full stomach whilst his neighbor goes hungry is not one of us." *Zakat* given by individuals and families is often collected by large central funds that, in turn, distribute it to individuals in need or other organizations that ensure care of the needy and help establish and maintain Islamic social order. It is an institutionalized way of fighting against the establishments that give rise to societal injustices, such as poverty, poor education, and chronic unemployment. The Zakat Foundation of America, for example, is a nonprofit that collects *zakat* donations and uses the funds for various disenfranchised groups in the United States and around the world, such as the homeless, prisoners, and single mothers. Just one of the many things they do is distribute one thousand backpacks and school supplies each year to children in the United States who are living in poverty.

Whether or not we consider our giving specifically a form of *zakat*, this Muslim practice underscores the importance of understanding that our giving can shape not only our personal identity, but the identity of an entire community.

CHRISTIAN TITHING—A HOLY HABIT

When I teach classes on faith and giving and we talk about giving out of obligation, the topic of the tithe always arises. People have surprisingly strong feelings about it, and the particularities of the practice always seem to be in question, perhaps because tithing lacks clearly delineated guidelines. Some people say tithing is a biblical principle that is required by God. Some large, high-profile churches, for example, have even incorporated tithing as a requirement for church membership; new members are asked to sign a covenant that includes giving 10 percent of their income to the church.

Others debate whether one should give away 10 percent of income or wealth. And if the answer is income, is it gross or net? Is the tithe calculated before or after taxes? And is the remaining 90 percent free for us to do with as we want? If tithing is giving 10 percent of my money, is giving of my time and giving of myself less important? Is 10 percent for the poor the same as 10 percent for the middle class or the rich? Some even argue that the tithe was something practiced only in biblical times with no relevance today. The debate seems endless.

But becoming bogged down in the minutiae of the tithe—or any obligatory form of giving—misses the bigger picture. Approaching such an obligation with a minimalist mindset—What's the minimum I can do and still fulfill the obligation?—keeps you locked into narrow ways of thinking and makes becoming a generous soul that understands and experiences the joy of giving that much more difficult.

The reality is that, despite all the debate, only a small percentage of people actually give away ten percent of their income. Giving USA, the popular annual report on American philanthropy, calculates that individual giving as a share of personal income since 1965 has averaged around 2 percent per year.[3] When we look at giving as a percent of income within various Christian denominations, the average is again around 2 percent of income.[4]

In my workshops I like to suggest that such debates about tithing are more often than not the wrong conversations to be having because they focus primarily on the incidental details behind tithing. At the heart of such debates is the fundamental question, How much do I *have* to give? A more transformative way of thinking about the issue is to ask instead, How much do we need to *keep*? What if we used our 10 percent tithe, or our *zakat* (alms tax), or our *tzedakah* (righteous giving), not as the upper limit of our giving but rather as a benchmark and a starting point? What if we saw tithing within a greater framework of spirituality, as a means to an end—generosity being the end? Tithing is a technique we can use to shape our lives as generous beings who reflect God's bounteousness and live out our place within the sacred economics of this world. If we approach our obligatory giving not as some kind of divinely ordained quota but rather as a tool to help motivate us to give when our desire is waning, we might be changed into people who give intentionally and freely under many different circumstances from a life of generosity.

While most religions encourage obligatory giving, being motivated to do philanthropy out of obligation doesn't have to be a spiritual undertaking. Aristotle, for example, wasn't religious but saw giving as obligatory. He said, "Givers are called generous.... They give to the right people, the right amount, at the right time ... because that is the noble thing to do." Some would argue we have the responsibility as citizens of this world to give to one another, as a reflection of our common humanity. Under this more civic understanding, nineteenth-century English medical missionary Sir Wilfred T. Grenfell said, "The service we render to others is really the rent we pay for our room on this earth. It is obvious that man is himself a traveler; that the purpose of this world is not 'to have and to hold' but 'to give and serve.'"

Here are some ways to start and maintain obligatory giving:

- Write down why you feel it is your duty to give. Are you motivated by a particular piece of scripture? A lesson passed on to you from a parent? Put this statement with your budget as a reminder for when you plan your spending, saving, and giving.
- Establish a percentage of income to give away this year that you know you can achieve. Aim to increase that by one percentage point each year.
- One way to hold yourself accountable is to make a commitment to an organization. Some local faith communities and nonprofits take pledges in order to plan each year's budget. Pledges are paid off throughout the year, not necessarily in one bulk payment. The organization you have pledged to will often send you reminders in the mail or electronically about how much you have pledged to give, a simple form of accountability.
- Remember, obligatory giving isn't about meeting a minimum requirement. While you want to hold yourself accountable to the minimum you have set, you also don't want to miss out on opportunities to give over and above that. One way to do this is to direct one small source of income directly to your giving—the change you collect each day from your pocket, the money you get from recycling your aluminum cans, the cash you make from a garage sale. Why not set that money aside to go directly toward your extra-abundance to be given away?

PITFALLS OF OBLIGATORY GIVING

Following the path of obligatory giving can lead us to transformed selves, but adopting a posture of "I *should* give" also leaves us open to some unique pitfalls. One of these is that we may not be as diligent or intentional in determining where and when to give. For example, there will always be some religious and spiritual leaders whose motivations for requesting money are less than noble, and who will prey on your sense of obligation to wrest funds from you that will largely line their own pockets. These people often display a skillful manipulation of your fear and guilt, combined with some grandiose promises about how God will reward you for your gift. Some even develop a whole theology around money. I have heard certain pastors use scriptural verses such as 2 Corinthians 9:6—"The one who sows bountifully will also reap bountifully"—to support provocative claims that giving lavishly is a kind of divine investment: the more money you give to his or her ministry or cause, the greater the financial return God is certain to bestow back upon you. In Christian circles, this is often known as the prosperity gospel.

If someone plays on your sense of guilt or fear to give, it's a good sign that they're running a scam. On the other hand, someone pointing out your moral responsibility to act in accord with your beliefs is another matter.

This happened to me when I was a college student. Tony Campolo, a sociologist and former college professor, and a liberal evangelical Christian, was speaking at an event I attended. An offering was being collected to support missionaries stationed around the world, and Campolo said a few words before the collection began. I was a student and had little money, so I basically tuned out everything he was saying and made up my mind just to pass the plate right on by. But then Campolo caught my attention: "I have good news and bad news," he said. "The good news is we've already raised our goal of ten thousand dollars for the poor. The bad news is, it's in your pockets." He was exactly right. His words struck a chord deep in me that urged me, as a person who claimed to care about the poor, to live up to what I thought were my convictions and take action, however small, to help make real what I had only talked about. His challenge to us—to me—that night was just the nudge I needed to act. Despite my small, student-size budget, I proudly wrote a check that evening for an amount that forced me to sacrifice. It wasn't much when compared to the ten thousand dollars he wanted to raise, but for me it was huge. That was the first time I had given a substantial amount of money away, and for the first time I felt like I was a part of something much bigger than myself. I had begun the journey of transformation.

Giving out of obligation can also backfire. When you self-consciously fulfill an obligation, your focus may remain on you and the good deed you are doing. In this equation, the receiver of your gift can be reduced to little more than a required element in the act of your charity—the pitied or overlooked recipient of your grand gesture of noblesse oblige.

> "Giving simply because it is right to give, without thought of return, at a proper time, in proper circumstances, and to a worthy person, is enlightened giving. Giving with regrets or in the expectation of receiving some favor or of getting something in return, is selfish giving."
>
> (Bhagavad Gita 17:20–21)

I remember as a young teenager going on a mission trip to rebuild the home of a low-income woman whose house was mangled by a hurricane. I wasn't motivated to participate for any overwhelmingly altruistic reason. My church told me it was the type of thing we should do—it was an obligation—so some of my friends and I signed up to go. I felt good about myself for doing something so saintly as construction for the poor, but during that week of hammering and painting, I failed to even really notice the person inside the house. Her name was Mrs. Wheeler, and she was the grandmother of eight children, but I didn't see her as a real person; a few times I even forgot her name! She was just another feature of the landscape, something necessary for me to accomplish my good and selfless deed.

I completely missed the point of the trip. I had made the event about me and, in doing so, turned Mrs. Wheeler into an object. Sacred giving is just as much about how we treat the receiver as it is about what we are giving in the exchange. When we give, the receiver deserves our respect. In fact, Hindu leader Swami Vivekananda taught that we should be thankful for the very presence of the receiver, not out of pity, but out of appreciation:

> Do not stand on a high pedestal and take 5 cents in your hand and say, "here, my poor man," but be grateful that the poor man is there, so by making a gift to him you are able to help yourself. It is not the receiver that is blessed, but it is the giver. Be thankful that you are allowed to exercise your power of benevolence and mercy in the world, and thus become pure and perfect.[5]

When you give, ask yourself, "How can I best preserve the dignity of the receiver?" Recipients of gifts usually want to feel empowered too. For example, Habitat for Humanity has the families they help put in what they call "sweat equity," a number of hours spent helping to construct their own home, so that they feel like an integral part of the process.

ACTIONS LEAD TO FEELINGS LEAD TO TRANSFORMATION

Obligation is a tough sell, so I am not surprised if some of you haven't jumped on the commandment train quite yet. But hang in there with me; there really is more to it than just "do it because God says so." I am as hard-headed as they come, and if anyone tells me to do something I hunker down and refuse to move. But practicing a spiritual discipline out of obligation is not just following an authority out of blind obedience; rather, it is allowing God to shape us in a particular way and then acting out of that identity. For stubborn people like me, obligatory acts also offer that extra push that's sometimes needed. When I am stubbornly refusing to participate in an activity, about the only thing that gets me moving is knowing I am obligated to participate.

I'm reminded of physical education class in middle school. There is a special place in heaven for middle school PE teachers, but I digress. I disliked middle school gym class with more passion than my disgust for turnip greens, family reunions, and yearbook photos combined. Every day I would debate the merits of PE. Since there were no positives in my mind, the "debate" was more like a soliloquy on how silly the class was. But as the bell rang, I knew I had no choice whether or not I would participate. Unlike the rebellious girls who sat out of class when the mood struck them to not perspire, my formation as a good student and responsible teen motivated me to participate. My obligation to follow the rules was the extra push I needed to get me moving.

In addition to gym glass, I also rely on obligation when it comes to befriending peculiar neighbors, paying my taxes, and going to the dentist. These are areas of my life in which I tend to cling strongly to my own desires—ignoring people I find odd, not giving money to a government that seems so often to waste it, and not having sharp metal objects poking around my teeth. But obligation motivates me to participate in these activities that are ultimately worthwhile. For many people, giving is one of these activities. If that is true for you, get ready for a little holy motivation. When we're willing to follow certain spiritual practices, by choice or by force, God forms us to be more like God. We have the opportunity to be shaped into the best possible versions of ourselves. In those moments when giving is the last thing you want to do, let your motivation come from God in the form of obedience to a sacred obligation.

There is beauty in obligatory practices because the mandatory act grows out of a person's religious identity. As a Christian, being generous is part of who I am as a follower of God. In many ways it's not even a choice I make. Even when I don't want to practice generosity, I do it anyway because it's part of being me; it's part of my story. Stanley Hauerwas, named America's Best Theologian by *Time* magazine in 2001, taught me this concept. He says:

> Liberalism, in its many forms and versions, presupposes that society can be organized without any narrative that is commonly held to be true. As a result it tempts us to believe that freedom and rationality are independent of narrative— that is, we are free to the extent that we have no story.[6]

People of faith have religious narratives that free us to live out our stories in obedient acts such as giving. This is good news to many folks. But then people still question: "Does it even count if my heart really isn't in it?"

The answer is yes, it counts. While feeling a desire to give can be an important motivating factor, the lack of emotion does not make the practice any less authentic. And if giving is an obligation in your tradition, lacking the desire to give doesn't exempt you from your practice. In fact, lack of emotion is all the more reason to embrace the obligation, for that is its purpose— to get us to do something that is important and good for us, even when we don't *feel* like doing it. Even having mixed motives does not negate the merit of giving. I particularly like this from the Talmud, "If a person says, 'I am giving this coin to charity so that my child will live,' or 'so that I will make it into the next world,' he is regarded as completely righteous (his self-centered motives notwithstanding)" (Talmud *Pesachim* 8a–b).

In the words of poet Walt Whitman, "The habit of giving only enhances the desire to give." As with any spiritual discipline, we may start practicing giving out of obligation, but once we begin to see how our perspective is changed and broadened, the obligation turns into genuine desire. After a while, we become transformed and no longer have to make such deliberate and intentional choices about whether or not to act; instead, we act without thought because it flows from this new-found identity. My ultimate goal is to be formed into a person of generosity, not just a person who practices individual acts of generosity out of obligation. But in order for that to happen, I must regularly participate in acts out of obligation to train my desires. These acts shape reality over time and transform my identity. Generosity then becomes something that's "just what I do" as a child of God, not "something I consider doing" when an opportunity presents itself. The act of giving, ultimately, shapes me into who God created me to be.

As we grow in our giving, we learn to give in different and more mature ways. A number of people have identified levels of giving that are helpful as benchmarks for growth. The oldest and most well-known hierarchy was created by medieval Jewish philosopher Moses Maimonides. Commonly referred to as Maimonides' Ladder, the hierarchy lists eight levels of how to distribute *tzedakah* (righteous giving), with the top rung being the most desirable form of giving. This ancient rubric still resonates as a guide for us today. First, read the ladder and see on which rung you find yourself. Be honest, but also be kind to yourself. Remember that any giving, even if you have mixed motives, has merit. At the same time, see what more advanced rungs appeal to you. Can you envision engaging in that kind of giving yourself? What would it take to achieve that? What's stopping you?

> 8. *One who assists a poor person by providing him with a gift or a loan or by accepting him into a business partnership or by helping him find employment—in a word, by putting him in a situation where he can dispense with other people's aid*. For example, teaching a person a trade, finding them a job, lending money to help the person become self-supporting, teaching them to fish. Anything to help a person escape the cycle of poverty.
>
> 7. *One who gives alms to the needy in such a way that the giver does not know to whom he gives and the recipient*

does not know from whom he takes. You donate money anonymously to a charity that educates children in poverty without any restrictions for how the money should be used.

6. *The giver knows to whom he gives, but the poor person does not know from whom he receives.* You arrange to have a family's electric bill paid for the month, but you make sure they don't find out it was you who did it.

5. *The poor person knows from whom he is taking, but the giver does not know to whom he is giving.* You donate money, publicly in your name, to a local charity that provides food and shelter for the homeless.

4. *Someone gives the poor person a gift before he asks.* You offer to take a young single pregnant woman in your community on a shopping trip to prepare for her baby's arrival. She doesn't ask you to do it; you antici-pate her need. But you also risk that she might feel shame for being seen as needy.

3. *One who gives only after the poor person asks.* Walking through the park, you pass a homeless man sitting on a bench. If he stops and asks you for money, you're happy to give him some. But if he doesn't say any-thing, you're happy to keep walking.

2. *One who gives less than is fitting, but does so with a friendly countenance.* You're happy to support the fire-fighters who are collecting money at the major inter-section in town. You role down your car window and gladly put a few dollars in the boot. But the truth is, you could have easily given more.

1. *One who gives ungraciously.* This may be your reaction when a friend or coworker's child asks you to buy a magazine subscription to help support the marching band. You don't want another magazine, and you

don't even like the band. So, you role your eyes a bit as you give the kid a check.[7]

Maimonides' Ladder is helpful for a few reasons. First, it reminds us that creating a lifestyle of generosity is a process, not an overnight achievement. There are steps and, as with learning any skill, we get better as we go. Second, Maimonides' rungs show us that the motivation and attitude behind a gift is as important, if not more important than how much we give. Growing in generosity is not just about adding zeros to our end-of-the-year totals; it's about how the gift passes from our hands to another's.

BEYOND MONEY AND BEYOND OBLIGATION

Maimonides' Ladder also intimates another crucial aspect of obligatory giving—namely, that nonfinancial giving is also important. In fact, his most advanced form of giving expressly includes other types of giving, such as sharing your time and teaching your skills to others.

The traditions we've looked at in these chapters also acknowledge the importance and efficacy of nonfinancial giving. In Judaism, another concept similar to *tzedakah* (righteous giving) is *g'milut chasadim* (performing acts of lovingkindness, such as burying the dead). This type of giving, however, is broader in scope than rendering monetary or material assistance but is also about generosity.

In Islam, a form of voluntary giving known as *sadaqah* is giving over and above the 2.5 percent minimum represented by *zakat* (alms tax). Whereas the distribution of *zakat* is managed by a central authority, *sadaqah* can be given by an individual directly to the recipient; and while *zakat* is only monetary aid, *sadaqah* can be a gift of money, time, or even just a smile.

Such nonfinancial giving, or giving over and above what is required, also results in a range of benefits for the giver as well as the receiver. Some of these are hopes for benefits in the life after this one—"storing up rewards for yourself in heaven," so to speak. *Sadaqah*, because it is voluntary, is thought to count generously toward your rewards in the hereafter. Judaism points to Proverbs 10:2 and 11:4: "Charity saves from death." In Hinduism, giving is known as *dana*, and it is a way to purify your life. We are told: "He who gives liberally goes straight to the gods; on the high ridge of heaven he stands exalted" (*Rig Veda* 1.125.5).

But the rewards are not only in the afterlife. Besides a changed perspective and a transformation into a person of generosity, various scriptures do indicate that we might receive some unexpected blessings in this world as a result of our generosity. In the Qur'an we read: "Those that give alms, be they men or women, and those that give a generous loan to God, shall be repaid twofold. They shall receive a noble recompense" (Qur'an *Al-Hadid* 57:18). The Islamic text also says: "Anyone who is stingy, is stingy only with his own soul. God is wealthy while you are poor" (Qur'an *Muhammad* 47:38). In other words, to not give means missing out on the blessings. Or to quote a common Christian text on the rewards of giving: "Give, and it shall be given unto you; good measure, pressed down, and shaken together, and running over, shall men give into your bosom. For with the same measure that ye mete withal, it shall be measured to you again" (Luke 6:38). The Jewish community looks to Proverbs 19:17: "He that is gracious to the poor lends to God and his good deeds He [God] will repay him."

Above all, a life of generosity is the result of obligatory giving. You can be transformed into a generous giver, not just a person who gives generously, thanks to practices such as *tzedakah* (righteous giving), *zakat* (alms tax), and the tithe. But practices don't have to be about money. Here are some nonfinancial things you can do to promote giving as a holy obligation:

- Set up a schedule to volunteer with a local charity on a regular basis. Tutor children after school, direct people to rooms at the hospital, serve meals at a soup kitchen, take care of animals at a shelter. By committing to a schedule, you will have a sense of accountability.

- Commit to a particular generous practice: "Every time I encounter _____, I will _____." For instance, every time I encounter another driver who needs to be let into traffic I will stop and let the person in. Or, every time my friend Mary calls and needs to talk, I will make time to listen.

- Create a regular agenda item on your calendar to call or write someone—a sick friend, a neighbor in grief, a nervous new mom. I love writing letters to my grandmother who lives in an assisted-living facility now and loves hearing from her grandchildren, but I often simply forget or allow other things to get in the way. So, for a couple years I've been making appointments on my calendar to "call or write Gram." Writing it on my calendar reminds me to do it, makes it a priority, and increases its importance.

- Brainstorm as a family a list of things you could do to give to the environment—use cloth instead of paper napkins, take a reusable mug to the coffee shop, use cold water for washing clothes, unplug appliances and electronics when not in use, keep the air at a more moderate level. Now, as a group, choose which ones you want to agree to do and write them on a piece of paper. Sign the piece of paper and put it on the fridge or somewhere everyone can see it. In a few months, try some new things.

- Educate yourself on a topic that you are interested in—health care, migrant workers, animal welfare, renewable energy, nutrition in schools—by collecting reading materials on your nightstand. Then read about the subject for five minutes every night. In a month, you will be much more aware of the issues at stake and more ready to efficiently help in a hands-on way.

- Plan a regular lunch date with a friend. As part of your excursion, stop by the blood bank together and give blood.

FROM OBLIGATION TO TRANSFORMATION

When I am stubbornly refusing to participate in an activity, about the only thing that gets me moving is knowing I am obligated to participate. But obligation motivates me to participate in these activities that are ultimately worthwhile. For many people, giving is one of these places. When we're willing to use whatever wealth and possessions we retain in holy and life-giving ways, by choice or by obligation, God forms us to be more like God. In turn, our entire lives become an act of generosity, and we have the opportunity to be shaped into the best versions of ourselves possible.

CHAPTER FOUR

GIVING AS REDEMPTION

Restoring Money as Life-Giving Legal Tender

redeem—*to buy back; to free what distresses or harms; to change for the better*
—Merriam-Webster Online Dictionary, www.m-w.com

Sophocles once wrote, "Money: There's nothing in the world so demoralizing as money." For many of us, thoughts of money only conjure up issues of stress, angst, and inadequacy. How will I pay for my children's college education? Where will we get the money to pay for this month's mortgage? My car needs to be fixed and it's another week before I get a paycheck. Money is a reality that we all live with and a reality that can very easily control our lives. An Associated Press poll in November of 2006 found finances to be the number one cause of stress for people in the United States. Some people even associate money with iniquity and vice, appealing to the apparent wisdom in the aphorism, "Money is the root of all evil."

It is true that financial worries have a profound power to drain the joy right out of our lives. And yet, money is just a thing; by itself, it is neither good nor evil. The aphorism, "Money is the root of all evil," as we noted earlier, is actually a common misquote of a verse from the Bible that reads, "The *love of* money is a root of all kinds of evil" (1 Timothy 6:10). The difference is important to note, for though our experience of money may be life-robbing, it doesn't have to be. In fact, money can be redeemed—by which I mean money can be used as a tool to celebrate life and increase joy rather than being a source of contention or stress. The key is to have a proper, skillful relationship with money—neither fearing it nor craving it, but respecting it and the power it can have in our lives and in the lives of others. You may not be surprised that one effective way of achieving and maintaining a healthy relationship with money is by giving, for in the transaction, we reorder our priorities and expectations and learn to treat money with a lightness of spirit, and we discover the inherent worth—not the financial value— of things in our lives.

In fact, through skillful giving, money can be transformed from a profane object into a sacred tool for achieving good. But before we discuss that, let's first look at how our attitude toward money can influence our experience of life.

MONEY DOESN'T CREATE HAPPINESS; IT DULLS LIFE

A common theme in our cultural clichés and pop culture phrases is, "Money can't buy happiness," or, "Money can't buy me love." Yet over and over again we fight against the tendency to purchase pleasure. It's so tempting because for at least a nanosecond the excitement and variety of having something new makes us think we're experiencing true happiness. But when a few weeks or months pass and we're bored and want the next version or model, it's clear that what we experienced wasn't real happiness after all. Studies show us that the Maasai herdsman of East Africa are just as happy as the incredibly rich people on the Forbes 400 list.[1] This research doesn't downplay the deprivations of poverty—far from it. It just means that pursuing money for the sake of happiness doesn't get you very far. You just chase your own tail always trying to get more and more.

Money used to constantly consume and hoard can not only turn us into gluttons for possessions, it can dull our experience of life. Worries about money have the power to dull our lives in such a way that there is no color, no music, no laughter. The moment we wake up we forget to be thankful for our partner waking up right beside us; instead we're grouchy because the mattress sags in the middle and it's too expensive to replace. On our morning drive we fail to notice the huge banner outside our office building wishing us a happy birthday because we're busy noticing the brand new Lexus that the person we supervise just got; how can they afford that? And over dinner, our children's laughter is overshadowed by the phone ringing, another bill collector.

SELLING OBJECTIFIES: MONEY AND THINGS

Almost everything in our culture today can be exchanged for a certain amount of money; everything is for sale. I recently spent half an hour browsing a popular Internet auction site and found all manner of things for sale: advertising space on pregnant bellies, a blue toothpick, a DVD with scratches and smudges in the shape of Jesus, pheromones that promise to attract the opposite sex, a ghost in a jar. And it's not just the Internet doing the no-holds-barred selling. Fashion magazines hawk an amazing array of beauty products that are purported to make you irresistible. Television assaults you at every moment with ads for products that will solve any dilemma—blue pills for a good sex life, the right case of beer to make your friends love you, diamond earrings to solve a marital squabble. Some parents enroll their children in prestigious and wildly expensive preschools, hoping an early advantage will parlay into more advantages later in life. Beauty, friendship, sex, even success—we have managed to put a specified *value* in the form of a price tag on everything, and set it within the framework of the American marketplace.

This marketplace culture objectifies our possessions and reduces them to mere "things" that can be bought and sold. It also minimizes any real relationship we have with the items themselves and possibly with the person with whom we engage in the transaction. When we treat possessions and money this way, even our relationships are reduced to an objective measure. Perhaps this is why the old advice "never lend money to friends or family" is so sage.

But what effect does this marketplace culture have on our lives? Reducing almost anything to a financially quantifiable amount is convenient from an economic standpoint, but such focus on value alone exacts a toll on us, leading to envy, self-criticism, and other negative emotions. For example, if I can find a buyer to exchange $200,000 for my house, but my next door neighbor's house will fetch $275,000, it's tough to convince myself that her house is not better somehow because hers is "worth" more. Never mind that the only reason her property has more value at a particular time is because her buyer happens to share her passion for 1970s-era green shag carpeting and a garish salmon-pink paint job in most rooms. Never mind that I happen to adore my house because the layout is spacious and fits my particular lifestyle just right. I can't help but feel envious, even if just a little bit. The value of the neighbor's house trumps the worth of mine to me. In reality, her house was valued higher because of a particular set of peculiar circumstances. But in becoming envious, I have tacitly inserted myself into a kind of social stratification that blurs the lines between value and worth.

The same is true about salaries. I find it very hard not to judge my worth based on the amount of money I earn. Compensation is the value that someone assigns to our services, but, again, most of us confuse this number with self-worth, which results in anxious questioning—Who makes more than me? Who makes less than me? I am embarrassed to admit I feel better about myself if I know I make more than someone else, because I feel somehow that *I* am somehow worth more than that other person. But is this really so surprising? Our society places a tremendous amount of value on sell-ability. How much are you worth if you add everything up—your car, your clothes, your house, your career services? We compare ourselves to others based on these values. Real-estate mogul Donald Trump isn't ashamed to admit he subscribes to this notion: "Money was never a big motivation for me, except as a way to keep score."

Engaging this paradigm of value in the form of mindless consumerism also causes us to become objects of sorts. In my most unhealthy moments I turn to shopping as a way to lift depression. In those times, I find myself hopping from store to store filling my bags full of stuff that will "make me feel better." But the truth is, with each store I enter the shopping becomes more and more of an out of body experience. I'm going through the motions, but I'm not feeling a thing. Consuming dulls our souls as it turns everything into objects and turns us into vessels of utilization. Money captures and takes hold of our imagination so that the best idea we can come up with to cure our ailments is a set of high-thread-count Egyptian cotton sheets. This kind of consumption only serves to ensconce us in isolation.

The objectification of things through the process of selling, buying, and otherwise assigning financial values also can act nefariously to undermine our intuitive understanding that what's more important is what something is inherently worth, which is a far more subjective, even subversive, thing. Consider ways in which you might engage mindlessly in this kind of objectification process. How can you work against fearing or craving money?

- You find yourself daydreaming about personal finances—worrying about how you're going to pay for this, that, or the other. Set aside a time each week when you work on paying bills, referring to your budget, making financial decisions. If you find yourself getting anxious over money issues throughout the week, write them down in a journal and then let them go. During your appointed weekly time you can refer back to what you've written and deal with the concerns then.

- It's almost impossible to notice how much we are exposed to advertisements. There are the obvious—billboards, magazines, television commercials—and the not so obvious—contestants drinking a certain brand of soda on a reality show, a celebrity wearing a particular designer jean in public, young people talking up new bands on the streets and in subways so those passing by will overhear. Have fun with your kids and see how many ads—both obvious and nonobvious—you can identify in a day. Being aware of how you are being marketed to will give you agency as companies try to subversively dictate what you buy.

- Do you turn to buying when you're having a bad day or when you're not feeling good about yourself? Sometimes it's hard to tell. Consider keeping a journal for a month about how you feel. It can be as simple as drawing a happy, sad, or neutral face for each day. Also keep your receipts. Then go back and compare how you were feeling and when you tended to spend money. For me, there is typically a correlation, so I have a simple rule for myself: I can buy it … tomorrow. No more spur-of-the-moment spending for me.

- Many faith communities designate one day of the week as Sabbath—a day to rest. In keeping, many people do their best not to shop on these days to allow businesses to close and to avoid dealing with money altogether. Think about what it would look like for you to practice Sabbath in this way. You would have one day a week to not worry about money or get worked up over craving stuff to purchase.

- Go back to the budget that you worked on in chapter 2. Look at the categories of items and where you spent more money than you expected. What's behind the excessive spending? What cultural narratives were you listening to when you spent hundreds of dollars on hair-care products? "The fuller and shinier your hair, the more the opposite sex will like you." What was really behind all the cash that went toward the top-of-the-line television? "A big television is a sign that I'm successful." These messages aren't obvious at the time, but in hindsight we can dig out deeper meaning.

GIVING SUBJECTIFIES: MONEY AND EXPERIENCES

Most faith traditions teach that all things are from God and made in the image of God and therefore have an innate worth that does not fluctuate. My own religious tradition teaches that I have profound, inherent worth as a human because I am a child of God, a God who loves us subjectively, not a God who views us as objects to be measured or placed within a pecking order of value. The significance of this truth in everyday life is that I can affirm that the labels on my clothes or the number of tools in my basement do not determine my worth. I am worthwhile because of *me*, not because of anything external to me that may increase or decrease my perceived value in the workplace or anywhere else in the world.

If selling objectifies a thing by reinforcing its value, giving that same thing away subjectifies it by affirming its inherent worth, translating it from the realm of the marketplace to the realm of the interpersonal. By definition, a gift is something voluntarily transferred by one person to another without compensation; so when we give a gift we do not predetermine an item's worth and then ask for that amount in exchange.

This act of giving is in itself radically opposed to the value-assigning, market-driven, objectifying culture we live in. Author and pastor Lloyd Shadrach said it well: "Generosity is to materialism what kryptonite is to Superman." It fights against the powerful notion that everything is for sale and everything has a price. When we give something away, we very well may be aware of the approximate value of the thing, but coming to a mutually agreed-upon value between giver and receiver is not necessary for the transaction to occur. As philosopher Jacques Ellul wrote, "Not only does (generosity) destroy the power of money, but even more, it introduces the one who receives the gift into the world of grace ... and it begins a new chain of cause and effect which breaks the vicious cycle of selling and corruption."[2]

Last year, my ten-year-old Toyota Camry started getting moody after a long road trip. I am a frequent traveler, and though I loved my car I had to acknowledge that the time had come to replace it. At the same time, a young guy in our church was in need of a car to drive to and from college. So, one Sunday afternoon he came over and drove away with a gift. The market value of my decade-old Camry was around $2,500, but by giving it away I actually increased the worth of the car both for me and the young man. I enjoyed giving him the car for many reasons: it saved me the hassle of selling it, I knew it would be used well, and I was able to meet someone's immediate and urgent need. And his gratitude for the gift of something he could not afford to buy for himself will carry forward in his own acts of generosity. If he had written me a check, the transaction would have been business, and little more. Instead, this act of giving forged a meaningful connection with another human being. By fighting against isolation, such connections help us get out of our own skin, enrich our experiences, and help us to engage wiser perspectives.

In my most healthy moments, I turn to giving instead of shopping to lift depression. Not long ago, I helped my mother-in-law put Christmas decorations on the tree, assisted the ladies at church with preparing baked goods for a fund-raiser, and gave a stranger bus fare, all in one day as deliberate acts of giving in order to help me out of a funk. The result was less glamorous than the glitz and thrill of the mall, but the result was healing and even reenergizing. I made genuine connections with other human beings and engaged with them in their joys and issues, which helped me gain perspective on my own. This connection is at the core of redeeming money and our attitudes toward it.

How might you find ways to turn to giving as an alternative to buying and as a way to subjectify your view of money and possessions?

- Have a media-free day to forget about consumption and to focus on others. Take a Saturday, for example, and turn off the computer, unplug the television, put away the magazines. Instead, spend the day with your family creating care packages for soldiers, baking cookies for the volunteer fire department, or cleaning up litter on a hiking trail.

- Online shopping can be particularly seductive when you're having a bad day or are lonely. To compensate, do your online shopping through a website where a portion of your online purchases goes to the charity of your choice. This won't magically lift you from your melancholy mood, but it can remind you of the needs of others and lessen the craving for more stuff.

- Weekend activities can add up—expensive concerts, fancy dinners, pricey tickets to the game. Even a simple movie with the family will set you back a pretty penny. It's hard not to get sucked into the trend to spend lots of money on your weekend entertainment, but remember that your personal worth is in no way related to your bar tab or the most expensive entertainment for your children. Try giving a night out to the parents of a newborn—baby-sit and treat them to dinner out.

Helping a new mom and dad for a few hours makes fretting over not having money to go out of town next weekend a little less dramatic.

- Vacations seem to get more extravagant and extreme every year; it's hard not to compare your trip to the state-park lodge with the vacations you read about celebrities taking on their private islands. Why not try a volunteer vacation? There are any number of organizations that send people on short-term excursions of service. Travel the world and help others while you're there—teach English, repair buildings, care for at-risk children. Or take a hiking vacation where you can clean and maintain the trails while enjoying being outdoors.

A Modus Vivendi of Giving Is Counter-Cultural

One reason giving has such potency to draw us out of ourselves and awaken us to new possibilities is because a lifestyle of generosity runs so contrary to prevailing attitudes about money and possessions. Consider the following quotations, some ancient and some modern, that sum up nicely very common attitudes in our day:

"Money alone sets all the world in motion."
—(Publilius Syrus)

"Money is the wise man's religion."
—(Euripides)

"You should always live within your income, even if you have to borrow to do so."
—(Josh Billings)

"Whoever said money can't buy happiness simply didn't know where to go shopping."

—(Bo Derek)

"I'm living so far beyond my income that we may almost be said to be living apart."

—(e. e. cummings)

"I've got all the money I'll ever need if I die by four o'clock this afternoon."

—(Henry Youngman)

"Anyone who lives within their means suffers from a lack of imagination."

—(Oscar Wilde)

"I was part of that strange race of people aptly described as spending their lives doing things they detest to make money they don't want to buy things they don't need to impress people they dislike."

—(Emile Henry Gauvreay)

"He who dies with the most toys, wins."

—(Popular bumper sticker)

All these folks seem to have been hoodwinked (at least for a while) into the vicious cycle of consumption—the more we buy, the more we want to buy more. It's no surprise really; we are constantly surrounded by advertisements, all convincing us we need the latest and greatest gizmo to make our lives better.

Lest we think that such expressions are merely poetic or quaint, let's look at some hard data that confirm that we as a society are deeply committed to hoarding everything—our time, talent, and treasure—for ourselves. For example, only one-third of Americans volunteer. While 67.3 percent of Americans give at least $25 annually, the average person who is philanthropic gives away $2,000, or 3 percent of their income. (Secular people give away, on average, 1 percent of their income; religious people give away 3 percent—2 percent to their faith community and 1 percent elsewhere.)[3] And consider how normal it is to have debt. According to Crown Financial Ministries, the average family spends $400 more than it earns each year, and 23 percent of the average person's net income goes toward paying existing debt (not including the mortgage on a home).[4] *Time* magazine reports that 14 percent of our disposable income is used to repay loans.[5]

Being countercultural means living or acting in such a way that resists or undermines the direction and accepted wisdom of the cultural mainstream, either as an individual or as a community. The Amish, teens abstaining from sex, nudist colonies—these are all groups of people doing things not considered "normal" in general society. But have you ever thought of giving as countercultural?

A modus vivendi (a lifestyle, a manner of living) of giving is not the practice of most people. Sure, most people typically practice some form of philanthropy every once in a while—dropping some coins in a charity collection box in a store, volunteering a few hours at their children's schools, or giving used clothes to a thrift store. But as we have discussed, those isolated acts of giving are very different from creating an entire lifestyle of generosity where we are intentional about what we do with all our energy, time, wealth, and belongings.

Living out generosity as a lifestyle isn't easy, not only because it's out of the mainstream, but because the voracious appetite of the cultural marketplace is ready to swallow us up at any moment. The more we consume, the greater our desire to consume becomes, not unlike craving more and more of a drug. Ben Franklin once said, "Money never made a man happy yet, nor will it. There is nothing in its nature to produce happiness.

The more a man has, the more he wants. Instead of its filling a vacuum, it makes one."

In our society, a majority of people are focused on pursuing the almighty dollar and get swallowed up. If we refuse to cooperate with culture and swim against the commodification stream, life doesn't have to be an exhausting rat race of consumption and debt. When we give—our time, talent, treasure—we practice the action most opposite consuming. Giving and receiving is the converse of buying and selling. Buying and selling is all about the consumer and feeding the economic engine. Giving and receiving is all about the "other" and sustaining humanity. Buying draws us away from others, as we accumulate more stuff and have less need for other people. Giving draws us into relationships and community and we interact with others and depend on them. We disconnect from the world when we consume; we reconnect when we give. Just as consuming more and more stuff shapes us into a particular identity, giving also forms us. The more we practice the art of giving, monetarily and otherwise, the more generous we become. Our eyes are opened to the needs of others, our grip on "stuff" becomes loosened, and our satisfaction comes from helping others, not amassing wealth.

A modus vivendi (a lifestyle, a manner of living) of generosity has the added benefit of inherently encouraging financial responsibility. We may spend money we don't have in order to treat ourselves to some luxury, such as a flat-screen plasma TV or a fabulous pair of pumps, but we are less likely to voluntarily accrue debt in order to give the money away. Hence, if we make giving a priority over spending on ourselves, we will naturally find our outgoing cash flow tempered.

Creating a lifestyle of giving is a way to push back against cultural norms that encourage us to be consumers and always want more. It is a way to redeem the use of money and possessions and restore our time spent on this earth to more than just consuming what's in front of us. Here are some practical things you can do to start developing your modus vivendi of giving:

- Make the choice to be downwardly mobile. In other words, choose to progressively downsize and simplify your lifestyle for the sake of having more funds to give to others. Instead of aiming toward a bigger house and a nicer car as you age, consider aiming toward being content with what you already have and not needing to increase. Even consider moving into a smaller home if you don't need that additional square footage. How might you cut back and funnel that savings toward others?

- Organize a project of giving that empowers others to give. From a one-time collection to creating an entire nonprofit organization, anything is possible. If there is a flood or hurricane in a neighboring town, organize a group to make flood buckets for those who face the task of cleaning up after a natural disaster. Or maybe you want to involve even more people; you might be the brain-child for the next life-giving charity. Nonprofits shouldn't be taken on lightly, but with measured caution they have the power to change the world.

- Teach your children to give. First, model philanthropy in your own life. Noted philanthropic physician Albert Schweitzer was famous for saying, "There are three ways to teach a child. The first is by example, the second is by example, and the third is by example." Second, find ways to involve your kids in a family's giving. Let them be a part of selecting the organizations your family supports. Bring them to the local senior center or humane society, where they can give the gift of their loving presence. Encourage them to divide their weekly allowance between three jars—save, give, and spend. Include the kids when making family financial decisions.

- Ponder what you do with your days—are you a paid career person, an unpaid parent, a part-time volunteer, a student, a retiree? Does your work—whatever it may be—fit within a lifestyle of giving? Whatever you do, do you feel like you're giving back to the world in some way? If not, how might you change that so that your work during the day is in line with a lifestyle of giving? It may be as simple as encouraging your employer to participate in some kind of community service. Or perhaps you feel it's time to switch careers.

A Final Word about Accumulating Wealth to Give It Away

Despite our tendencies to blame financial problems on the existence of money, money is not the real problem. It is how we use, possess, and cling to it that causes harm. Remember, the Timothy text says the *love* of money is evil. Or, to quote Gandhi: "Capital as such is not evil; it is its wrong use that is evil. Capital in some form or other will always be needed." Both the poor and the rich struggle to find rightly ordered understandings of money. Some succeed. In both poor and rich communities, we find individuals who have redeemed money from life-gripping green stuff to life-giving legal tender. They have found that the true worth of money is not its market value, what it can purchase for us, or the status it can earn us—but what it can do for someone else.

Hence, it is possible to accumulate large amounts of money without succumbing to the temptation to objectify it and risk the other dangers we have explored. It is, however, difficult to avoid the trap, for the amassing of money comes with unique responsibilities and temptations. "Whoever loves money never has money enough; whoever loves wealth is never satisfied with his income" (Ecclesiastes 5:10). Nevertheless, if our wealth is used altruistically, we can have a lot of fun by carefully making use of large sums of money for the sake of others.

Alan Slifka, Harvard Business School grad, successful businessman, and cofounder of the Abraham Fund, a nonprofit organization dedicated to promoting coexistence between Israel's Jewish and Arab citizens says, "Yes, I make money from my businesses, but the purpose is to give it away. Doing philanthropy—developing and supporting projects—is the reason I exist. Why work if not to make money to help other people?"[6] Slifka is using money as a tool for good. Clement of Alexandria, second-century teacher of the church, spoke of wealth as an instrument. He said, "Riches ... lie in our hand and are put under our power as material and instruments which are for good use to those who know the instrument. If you use it skillfully, it is skilful. Such an instrument is wealth. Are you able to make a right use of it?" Fourth-century saint John Chrysostom wrote, "How can the one who possesses wealth be good? One can only be good if one shares what one has with others." One example of this concept in action is John D. Rockefeller. As the first U.S. billionaire, Rockefeller had an unlikely outlook on his wealth:

> God gave me my money. I believe the power to make money is a gift from God ... to be developed and used to the best of our ability for the good of mankind. Having been endowed with the gift I possess, I believe it is my duty to make money and still more money and to use the money I make for the good of my fellow man according to the dictates of my conscience.[7]

As a Methodist, one of the people I look to the most in this area is John Wesley. As the founder of Methodism, Wesley was wealthy thanks to his preaching and teaching, but he died with only a small amount of money in his pockets and dresser. The man embodied generosity. He is famous for his saying, "Earn all you can, save all you can, and give all you can."[8] Slifka, Clement,

Chrysostom, Rockefeller, and Wesley all remind us that money is not an end; it is a means to an end.

The same is true of possessions. There is nothing wrong, in and of itself, with a desire for and ownership of material items; it's when you put your trust in these things and grip them so tightly, as if letting go would destroy you, that problems arise. One of the difficulties with wealth and possessions is that we try to protect our stuff. When we get so wrapped up in that protective role, it's hard to let go and give. French author André Gide wrote, "Complete possession is proved only by giving. All you are unable to give possesses you."

But again, a great responsibility comes along with being rich. "To whom much is given, much is expected" (Luke 12:48). So, you may not want to be rich; granted, you also probably would not choose to be poor. As the Proverb goes, "Give me neither poverty nor riches" (Proverbs 30:8). Frankly, it's all relative. There are such extremes of wealth and of poverty today that most of us land somewhere on the wealthy side of the center most of the time. God expects a lot from us in this position, but it's also an honor to be in a position where we can use the skills we enjoy to make money and then use that money to make other people live better lives. For some of us, the invitation to sacred giving may be earning a lot so that we can give a lot. If you choose to take this path, know that it's slippery; an abundance of wealth can quickly change a person's priorities. But it can be done and, as we have seen, the rewards are great. Whatever level of lifestyle we choose to adopt, God invites us to use money redemptively for the purpose of doing good in this world.

GIVING AS CHARITY

Providing for the Needy with Compassion

charity—*benevolent goodwill toward or love of humanity;
generosity and helpfulness especially toward the needy or
suffering*

—Merriam-Webster Online Dictionary, www.m-w.com

The words *charity* and *justice* are often casually thrown around
in the philanthropic vernacular, treated as synonyms in conversations about giving, or lumped together in faith communities as
some nebulous form of goodwill. But glossing over the distinc-
tions between these concepts and their rich economy of meaning
would mean missing out on some of the most profound opportunities for giving. Charity and justice *are* related, but they are
distinct in important ways. Hence, I have separated giving as
charity and giving as justice into our final two chapters to better
highlight how each can be an integral but distinct component in
our practice of giving.

First, let's establish basic definitions for each concept.
Charity, as I will be discussing it here, means doing good for
those who *need* something, such as providing groceries for a family living in poverty. Justice, on the other hand, means doing
good for those who are *owed* something, such as giving to organizations who work to ensure living wages for factory workers.
In terms of practice, charity is generally done for the sake of

individuals to meet *immediate* needs; justice is typically done for the sake of *groups* to change *systemic* issues. Moreover, acts of charity are done to address the *effects* of injustice; acts of justice are done to address the *causes* of injustice.

The best analogy I have ever heard to distinguish these ideas was written by temperance activist Joseph Malins in 1895.[1] As his poetic story goes, people were falling off a cliff, and the townspeople squabbled over whether to build a fence around the cliff or continue to send an ambulance down into the valley to rescue the fallen. Repair the effects or stop the cause? Charity or justice?

The answer, of course, is both—and sometimes it takes a truly catastrophic event to show that these related needs are both crucial to address. When Hurricane Katrina struck the Gulf Coast on August 28, 2005, thousands of people were driven from their homes and found themselves in immediate need of food, clothing, and shelter. Yet responding to these needs alone was not enough. These large groups of disenfranchised people also needed long-term, strategic assistance in the form of funds and personnel to rebuild the faulty levees, create better evacuation plans for the future, and examine why government assistance was slow in responding—and to implement changes at every level. Only by addressing issues of both charity and justice could true recovery from Katrina take root.

Some argue that giving as justice is a higher form of, or a greater moral obligation than, giving as charity, which is sometimes seen as ineffectual or at least inefficient. I disagree. While I do think charity is typically easier to practice than justice, both are needed and both are holy acts of giving. Our world needs those who will clothe the naked and feed the hungry directly, as well as those who will address the systems that create (or at least allow the existence of) unclothed and starving people. We need conservative communities that typically confront issues of charity and liberal communities that typically confront issues of justice. We need Republicans and Democrats. We need the Good Samaritans and the Prophets.

A simple medical analogy is apt. When I was a child, I got sick with bronchitis on an annual basis. My mother would give me an innocuous over-the-counter cold pill the size of a pea that did a great job of clearing up my symptoms. I felt so much better! But my mother also made me take antibiotic pills the size of grapes. I didn't understand this. Why go through the suffering of swallowing a horse pill when the other tiny little pill made me feel all better? The answer, of course, is because the small pill was only a temporary solution. It was an important part, however, because it kept me from being miserable and, in turn, making everyone around me miserable. (Oh how I loathed being sick as a kid; I've just never had the patience for snotty tissues and baritone coughs.) But only the antibiotics could get at the root of the problem and wipe it out. Two pills serving two purposes—both of which my body needed. Both of which our world needs.

It is worth noting here that giving as charity, as I am defining it, is different from supporting the arts, giving money to your alma mater, or contributing to a political party, which are (valuable) acts of civic philanthropy. Charity is primarily about helping those who go without food, clothing, shelter, or other necessities. Because charity is about engaging with the poor, the act invites us to step out of our own perspective for a time. Connecting with another person in this way is compassion. It is looking someone in the eye in an attempt to understand their world, to feel at least a bit of their pain, and to then be motivated to alleviate their suffering. Charity is *not* looking down on the needy with pity, feeling sorry for them, or thinking "there but for the grace of God go I." Instead, it is honoring these people by seeing them as complete human beings, seeing them without judgment, seeing them as God would see them.

Giving as charity is the most intimate and relational form of giving, and as such it has the most power to change who you are as the giver. More specifically, learning how to experience true compassion for "the other" (the poor, the disenfranchised, the marginalized) has been for me the most powerful step in attempting a lifestyle of generosity. If I could only choose one thing in this book to highlight, it would be the gift of compassion for those on the outskirts of society. I get excited just thinking about how the world could change through the power of compassion, so we will use this chapter to examine what it looks like to provide for another person's immediate needs via compassion—sitting with them in their darkest hours, carrying their burdens for a moment, and finding ways to lessen some of their suffering.

First, we will look at how charity can radically transform how you see the world and allow you to notice God in places you may have never imagined. Second, we will examine how direct, *face-to-face* giving in particular is a potent way of uncovering who you really are and what you really believe—to discover (and possibly begin to change) your very identity. But this kind of giving also brings with it some special dangers that can undermine these benefits. Keeping that in mind, we'll then look at these potential pitfalls and find ways to avoid them.

CHARITY TRANSFORMS YOUR POINT OF VIEW AND MAKES ROOM FOR THE SACRED

Having ourselves at the center of our point of view is natural to most of us. Why wouldn't it be? After all, day in and day out we engage in activities to meet our physical and emotional needs (eating, drinking, seeking friends) and in other activities to ensure our own well-being (working for a paycheck, taking care of our dwelling).

Such attention to our own health and happiness is only natural. But for most of us, this appropriate self-interest easily, and very often quietly, morphs into a kind of self-centeredness. This attitude can range from simple, benign thoughtlessness toward the needs of others, to more egregious and intentional forms of "me first" behavior. For example, I've spent a lot of time writing in local coffee shops and bookstores lately, and have come to think these places bring out people's ugly sides. I've seen patrons read stacks and stacks of magazines, not purchase them, and then leave them scattered on tables for employees or other customers to deal with. More troubling, I watched one woman get nasty with a barista because her triple-no-foam-latte was a few degrees hotter than she preferred.

Are these terrible crimes against humanity? No. But really—how difficult is it to put the magazine back in the correct slot on the shelf? Is it too much to ask to share your concern over too-hot coffee firmly but politely? All it takes is a bit of thoughtfulness and a measure of concern about what the *other person* might be feeling or needing. At the further end of the spectrum, you might find those who steal or lie or cheat—all in the name of getting ahead somehow, of putting their own needs before those of others.

But what if we flipped the focus and attempted to consider *you* before *me*. Former first lady Barbara Bush once said, "Giving frees us from the familiar territory of our own needs by opening our mind to the unexplained worlds occupied by the needs of others." Charity as giving, in particular, allows this change in perspective. To most effectively meet the needs of others, we must first sit alongside the recipient and understand their world. We have the opportunity to step outside the muck and mire of our own lives for a moment and walk alongside someone else—who, in turn, will walk with another one day, and on and on.

Try the following simple exercises—actually try them—and see if you begin to notice a shift in your point of view, from what's convenient for you to what will be helpful to others:

- Make eye contact with those you pass on the street and greet them with a smile. Even throw in a "hello" if you are in a part of the country where this won't be considered truly bizarre.
- Learn the name of someone whom you encounter on a regular basis but don't know personally (for example, a bank teller or mail carrier).
- Notice when a fellow driver needs to merge into traffic. No more looking straight ahead and acting like you don't see them. (I'm the worst at that.)
- When you're at the grocery store, put your shopping cart back in the rack and not in some random spot that's convenient for you. Not only can the cart dent someone's car, but an employee then has to spend extra time going around the parking lot collecting the carts. Even consider taking a wayward cart back into the store when you arrive for your shopping trip.

These are little things that don't take much effort and don't take us too far out of our comfort zone. They probably won't be the catalyst for world peace, but they will start re-forming you so that thinking about the needs of others isn't so foreign. And these small steps will build a foundation for transforming your paradigm through giving as charity.

Because charity allows you to see the world from a different point of view, it also allows you to encounter the sacred in ways you might not otherwise encounter it. This fundamental shift in perspective from ignoring or engaging "the other" in terms of what's in it for me (a point of view with you at the center) to what's in it for them (a point of view with them at the center) lies at the heart of encountering the Holy Other, a path recognized by so many of the world's spiritual traditions.

At the 2006 National Prayer Breakfast—an annual event since 1953 that is sponsored by Congress but organized by a secretive Christian organization known as the Fellowship—Bono, lead singer of the rock band U2, told the crowd, "Check Judaism. Check Islam. Check pretty much anyone … the one thing we can all agree, all faiths and ideologies, is that God is with the vulnerable and poor." Bono's references are on the mark. In the sacred text of Christianity, discussions of charity are hard to miss; there is an alarmingly large amount of scripture devoted to admonishments to take care of the needy. In the Bible, Jesus says:

> For I was hungry and you gave me food, I was thirsty and you gave me something to drink, I was a stranger and you welcomed me, I was naked and you gave me clothing, I was sick and you took care of me, I was in prison and you visited me.… Truly I tell you, just as you did it to one of the least of those who are members of my family, you did it to me. (Matthew 25:35–36, 40)

It's worth emphasizing that Christianity's sacred text understands that when you give to the poor, you are actually giving to *God*. In this way, giving charity is a doorway to encountering the sacred. When you spend time with the needy to learn about and meet their needs, you create space for a holy encounter and provide context for God to speak to you. I'm not talking about some kind of hocus-pocus thing where a rich person and a poor person meet, rub the magic lamp, and a genie appears to grant them three wishes from the Amazing Aladdin. This is not a magic formula. It is not a call to romanticize the poor or put them on a pedestal. Poverty is no cakewalk, and no one is perfect, including the poor people you are helping. But when you change your point of view and attend to the needs of others, particularly the marginalized, you are much more likely to notice the presence of the sacred than if you only focus on yourself.

Another transformation that happens when we encounter God through other people is that we realize we're more alike than different. Giving as charity can not only allow for a sacred encounter, but through that encounter you might discover that some of your preconceived notions about "those poor people" are wrong. With this realization, you will frequently discover a fresh compassion for, and different outlook on, all people—not just those in need of assistance. This, then, is the crux of the transformation offered by giving charity: seeing other people in such a way that you're able to see at least a speck of God in everyone.

So deeply rooted is this potential for transformation that many traditions make giving charity a form of obligation, such as we discussed in chapter 3. Pope Benedict XVI's first encyclical letter was about love as charity; he stated that giving charity is as important as two other foundational practices of the Roman Catholic Church, administering the sacraments and preaching the word. "The Church's deepest nature is expressed in her three-fold responsibility: of proclaiming the word of God (*kerygma-martyria*), celebrating the sacraments (*leitourgia*), and exercising the ministry of charity (*diakonia*)."[2] The Second Vatican Council, held in the 1960s, and later liberal theologians declared that scripture calls Christians to embrace a "preferential option for the poor."[3] The same conviction is felt in the Jewish tradition and reflected in the Hebrew Bible[4]—for example, Deuteronomy 15:11: "You shall open your hand wide to your brother, to your poor, and to your needy, in your land."

Indeed, giving as charity is transformative precisely when we understand with the eyes of faith that the needs of others lay claim to our abundance. "Generous people take upon themselves the fate of others," said French philosopher and Talmudic scholar Emmanuel Levinas. When I think about charity, I think about physical posture. To obtain a posture of giving, I first imagine arms outspread and hands open. To give something away, you can't clutch it tightly; your hands have to be open. Kabir (ca. 1398–1470), a great mystic and critic of religion and morality, said, "You came into the world with fists closed and you go away with open palms. So even while living stretch your hand open and give liberally."

WHAT CAN I DO?

Now that you understand the transformative power of charity, are you ready to get started? There are many things you can do right now to meet the urgent requests of those in poverty. Here are a few examples:

- The next time you stay at a hotel, save the travel-sized soaps and shampoos. Donate these to your local battered-women's shelter.
- Consider hiring a poor person at your workplace. Employment is a great gift. If you are not in the position of hiring in your line of work, consider paying the poor to do something around your home—clean your gutters, wash your windows.
- Give gently used business attire to a nonprofit organization that provides interview suits and professional support to low-income women or men.
- Donate money to organizations that fight global hunger.
- Volunteer with your local charities that help build homes for families in need.
- Go online and learn about the different social-service agencies in your community—food banks, women's shelters, homeless shelters, and the like. Find out what they need and where you could help.
- Buy your next pet at the local humane society instead of the local pet store.
- Donate items you no longer want or need to one of the many organizations that resell used clothing and household goods in their thrift shops.
- Keep fast food gift cards and bus passes in your car to give out to those asking for change on the street. This is a great

way to give them something without wondering how they will use the money. Also try to make yourself aware of local homeless shelters, battered-women's shelters, and other social service agencies so you can direct requests that you cannot fulfill. When you encounter a man or woman holding a "will work for food" sign choose to see him or her not as a nuisance but as a brother or sister, and as an invitation to connect with humanity and encounter the sacred.

Giving to the needy can sometimes be difficult simply because you fear being taken advantage of. I understand that fear, but I don't want that to stop you from the practice. Beth Templeton, who has spent twenty-five years working with homeless and poor people, offers some wise advice:

- Never do something for somebody that the person can and should do for themselves.
- Give money to vendors instead of the person.
- Verify the story before you pay a bill or help with a financial problem.
- Use a voucher system for food or gas.
- Don't believe everything you hear.
- You don't have to give people exactly what they want.
- Learn about available resources in your area and refer people to them.
- Explain the reason behind your answer to a request, and do not apologize.
- Never explain what an agency's policies are unless you are absolutely sure.

GIVING CHARITY FACE-TO-FACE REVEALS WHO YOU REALLY ARE

When you give as charity, you have two basic options—give to a charitable organization or give directly to an individual. In many

ways, the difference is how much interaction with the recipient
you want. While giving money to a charitable organization is
helpful, the most potent form of giving as charity comes in the
context of relationship—giving face-to-face with another
human being in need. When you give directly to another, you go
beyond imagining their perspective and actually enter into it—
even if only for a moment.

I want to emphasize that both approaches to giving charity
have positives and negatives. When we make a financial contribution to an organized charity, we miss out on forming a relationship with the needy and thereby miss out on uniting with
humanity on a deeper level. At the same time, you shouldn't feel
the need to reinvent the wheel every time you practice charity.
Philanthropic organizations provide you with a great way to
efficiently participate in curbing poverty; they can most likely
stretch your ten dollars further than you could on your own. For
these reasons, I always suggest a healthy mix, of supporting
organizations with established programs and forming your own
relationships, as a way to practice charity. One way to form personal relationships is to get involved with the organizations to
which you contribute funds.

Practicing charity face-to-face can be like standing naked in
front of a mirror. Most of us have a mental image of ourselves—
who we are, the kind of people we are deep down. But this self-
image often goes unchallenged until we find ourselves in—or
allow ourselves to enter—a position that's uncomfortable, where
we have to choose between two difficult options, and face crucial
questions about what we truly believe (not what we merely say
we believe). Such events are diagnostic moments for our souls.
Do we live up to our own ideals? Do we discover surprising
prejudices that we want to deny? On the other hand, do we find
courage we didn't know we had?

When we give charity directly to the recipient, we very
often enter into just such a diagnostic moment. For in that space

and time we enter into a direct relationship—however tenuous or brief—with the recipient, which is much harder and more courageous than writing a check to a faceless organization. Giving directly to flesh-and-bones people in dire, immediate need can shake things up.

For example, facing immediate needs often brings up uncomfortable questions. Do I believe that this person is telling me the truth? Just who do I trust, anyway? Will I be taken advantage of? If so, do I care? Is this safe? If I don't give, am I a bad person? What is my role in all this, anyway? What is God's role? Does this person *deserve* my money? Does this person *deserve* to be in dire straits?

Such questions may not be comfortable, but by honestly engaging them you come full circle and learn to discover your own identity—not the kind of person you want to be, or even necessarily the kind of person you think you are, but the kind of person you *actually* are. Seeing your true identity clearly is the first step in allowing for change into the kind of person you really do want to be.

A story from my own life can help illuminate some of these questions. A few months ago, a man named Marvin and his wife rang my doorbell looking to earn some cash by mowing the grass, cleaning the gutters, and so on. They explained how he had lost his job and that they had two kids back at home. Home for them was only a few blocks away from our house. My judgment kicked in and I became suspect of how people who lived in *my* neighborhood would end up knocking on doors for work. I remember acknowledging this thought and being so disappointed in this ugly side of myself.

Neither my husband nor I are fans of lawn care, so Marvin's offer was a nice excuse to pay someone to do yard work. Although, again, my ugly side came out when I assumed the quality of work would be under par because these people weren't part of my socioeconomic class. Not very flattering, Lauren.

Over the next few weeks, Marvin came back regularly, looking for more work. Each time he came riding a child's bike, and each time we would hear a little more about his life. The more I learned, the more "normal" he became to me. On about the fourth or fifth visit we started to run out of tasks. Nevertheless, the visits became more frequent. A couple of times we just gave Marvin money because he had immediate needs, such as buying asthma medicine for his child. I faced another moment in the mirror: does he really have a kid with asthma or is that just a good story? My husband and I decided to err on the side of trust and give him the money. I was slightly disappointed when Marvin's reaction didn't seem quite as grateful as I expected.

Later, we loaned Marvin a more substantial amount of money, which he said he wanted to pay back, and he promised to show up the next day to do some yard work. I was disappointed when he never did. But I still would loan him the money if I had it to do over again. I always say, "I'd rather be taken advantage of than play it safe," and I got to live that out.

I did not develop a deep friendship with Marvin, but we did form a relationship. Giving money to him was a qualitatively different experience than giving money to an impersonal poverty fund. This fund had a face; it had a story; and because it was human it disappointed me at times. But it also gave me the chance to see myself in a new light, warts and all. It changed me. Thanks to Marvin, I was exposed to deep-seated prejudices that can easily hide away in the dark reaches of my soul and serve only to limit my connection with humanity. Thanks to Marvin, I was reminded that poor people aren't these visions of perfection just waiting to accept your gift and grin from ear to ear.

Remember the story of me giving away my old car? We gave my old Toyota Camry to a college student we knew from the church where my husband was a pastor. The end of the story is that we never heard a word from him after that day. He didn't stop by the pastor's office with a plate of warm chocolate chip cookies. He didn't call to say thanks. He didn't send a note in the mail. Nothing. We haven't spoken a word to him or laid eyes on him since. Yet again, I saw my less flattering side come out as I thought, "Is he that ungrateful? Did he lie to us and sell the car for money?" Interacting with another human being in this way is a quick view into your own soul and sometimes a sobering reality check. For me, interactions with those I'm giving my money or other possessions to have been some of the most seminal life moments because I can't hide what I really think or who I really am. Just like being in the presence of God, sitting alongside those in need gives you the opportunity to be honest and change.

SOME DANGERS THAT CAN UNDERMINE CHARITY'S BENEFITS

As you prepare to practice charity, consider a few issues that will probably come up as you engage in giving to the needy. Instead of being surprised, think ahead about how you want to handle these situations.

TOO MUCH CONTROL

First, it can be tough as the donor to know how much control over the money you should retain. On one side of the coin, you might think, "It's my money and I'm responsible for making sure it gets used properly." On the other side of the coin, you might think, "My job is to give it away; I'd rather hedge my bets for the sake of generosity even if someone takes advantage of me." Whatever your thinking, be aware of either extreme. When we try to tightly control how our gift gets used, it is hard to avoid judging the person receiving the gift. And judging the recipient works directly against charity's ability to help you step outside your own perspective and be open for change, for an encounter with the sacred in others. Worry, judgment—these work against compassion.

There's a great German proverb: "Charity looks at the need and not at the cause." In other words, the point of charity isn't to figure out how the person got themselves into such a predicament to begin with. (Wait until the next chapter to worry about that.) Many faiths encourage you to let a higher power worry about the few bad apples who take donations and use them in unhealthy ways. Jewish tradition has a proverb that says, "If a man pretends to have a blind eye, a swollen belly, or a shrunken leg, he will not leave this world before actually coming into such a condition" (Talmud *Ketubot* 68a).

On the other hand, it is important to be wise when giving charity. If we casually give money to individuals and make no effort to inquire about their lives and why they need the money, we may unknowingly and unnecessarily enable substance abuse or encourage fraud. In Judaism, there is a wise tradition that says that if someone asks for clothes you investigate to make sure they are not a deceiving you, but if they ask for food you feed them immediately because they might die while you inquire about the truthfulness of their request.[5] Despite help from religious traditions, there are times when we get stuck, when we don't know the best thing to do—to give or not. When Marvin told us he needed money to buy his daughter asthma medicine, it was tough to know whether or not he was telling us the truth. But in that moment, we had to make a decision. We could either take the super-responsible route and not give him money because he might be using it to support a drug habit, or we could trust his story and give him money even though we didn't know for sure where it would go. As I explained, that night we opted for—and possibly erred on the side of—trust. In general, I typically go that way. I would rather someone question me for foolishly giving away too much money than for stingily keeping it because I didn't trust what people were telling me.

At moments like this, the sacred art of giving diverges from the secular art of giving. Noted philanthropist Andrew Carnegie, who wrote *The Gospel of Wealth*, adopted "scientific philanthropy" based on Darwin. He would completely disagree with me. In fact, he wrote "one of the serious obstacles to the improvement of our race is indiscriminate charity. It were better for mankind that the millions of the rich were thrown into the sea than to encourage the slothful, the drunken, the unworthy."[6] He believed we should only help those willing to help themselves. I believe in something more nuanced; I believe there is a divine power greater than me who plays a role in guiding my giving and in aiding those who receive my gifts. I certainly don't want to encourage or enable destructive behaviors by my giving, but I also don't want to play God in choosing how I dole out money.

PRIDE

A second situation can arise when you give to the needy: pride can easily creep in and steal your chance to experience deep connection with another person or with the sacred.

An old saying tells us, "It's not enough to do good; you must be *seen* doing good." This may be true if you're running for public office, but for the rest of us, nurturing a desire (however subtle) to receive acknowledgment (in whatever form) for our giving puts us back in the limelight and undermines giving's effectiveness in helping us see things from another's perspective. Giving charity isn't about me; it is about the other. So when giving charity becomes about me again, the process of transformation is thwarted.

To guard against turning the focus onto yourself, avoid making a big deal about your giving to others. From the Qur'an: "If you publish your voluntary offerings, that is good; but if you conceal them, and give them to the poor, that is better for you, and will acquit you of your evil deeds" (Qur'an *Al-Baqarah* 2:272). Consider declining the offer to put your name in a newsletter or other public notice. Even if you do receive recognition, deciding in advance that you will actively avoid it will help you receive it with true graciousness, and help prevent you from hoping for it the next time.

SHAME

Third, if we are not careful, giving charity to someone can accidentally embarrass that person by drawing attention to his or her poverty and need. From the Talmud: "It would have been better for you not to have given (the needy man) anything rather than giving to him (publicly), causing him embarrassment" (Talmud *Chagiga* 5a). Similarly, giving charity to someone can make him or her feel lesser than or of lower value as a person.

The key to avoiding this unintended embarrassment or shame is your intention. As givers, we have the opportunity not only to meet immediate needs, but also to empower the needy to become self-sufficient. You first give the starving person some fish to eat, but then, after he's eaten, you teach him how to catch some fish for himself. "One who lends money is greater than one who performs charity, and one who forms a partnership is greater than all" (Talmud *Shabbat* 63a).

We also have the power as givers to remind the needy that they are just as valuable, as human beings, as the rich—and that they, too, can participate in giving. Stories like the one found in Luke 21:1–4 remind us of the dignity that the needy receive from giving. In that story, Jesus witnessed a poor woman donating all the money she had to live on—"two small copper coins"—to the temple. Though her gift was small, Jesus declared that her gift was actually greater than the gifts of those donating much larger sums of money because it came from a sincere and devoted heart willing to sacrifice everything it had for the sake of others.

THE GIFTS OF CHARITY

When you practice charity through writing a check to an organization, as a result of creating a relationship, or by just spending time with the needy, you have the chance to connect deeply with both the wide expanse of humanity and the Sacred. You are able to shift the focus away from yourself and onto another person, creating a new point of view. This change in paradigm creates sacred space, as you celebrate the commonalities you share with those around you and take an introspective look at yourself. It is the entrenched prejudices we acknowledge in those moments of self-reflection that, over years and generations, give rise to societal injustices. In our final chapter we will explore how giving as justice can turn the tide and change the world.

GIVING AS JUSTICE

Believing in and Working toward
Righteous Equality

justice—*the act or practice of giving to others what is their due*

—Merriam-Webster Online Dictionary, www.m-w.com

The concept of justice has captivated thinkers, rulers, legislators, theologians, and everyday people for millennia. What's fair? What's right? What do people deserve, and why? To what degree should the government be involved in legislating social reform? Does everyone deserve financial security, or only those who work tirelessly for it? (What if you are not capable of working tirelessly or you work tirelessly at a job that doesn't even pay a living wage?) Should all people have the right to three meals a day, or only those who don't waste their money on nonessential things? (What if the disease of an addiction contributes to poor choices?) Is it necessary to treat all citizens with dignity, or just those who are law-abiding? (What if someone gets wrongly convicted of a crime? What if the experience of incarceration for a nonviolent offense incites a person to act aggressively after being released?)

Philosophies abound about the nature and role of justice in society, but the world's spiritual paths typically base their understanding of justice on the deceptively simple proposition that all people are fundamentally equal in the sight of God (created in the image of God in some traditions; equal in human potential in others). Consider the following excerpts from sacred texts:

"Have we not all one father? Has not one God created us?"
(Malachi 2:10)

"I look upon all creatures equally; none are less dear to me and none more dear."
(Bhagavad Gita 9:29)

"There is neither Jew nor Greek, there is neither slave nor free, there is neither male nor female, for you are all one in Christ Jesus."
(Galatians 3.28)

"All the people of the whole world are equally brothers and sisters. There is no one who is an utter stranger. There is no one who has known the truth of this origin. It is the very cause of the regret of Tsukihi (God). The souls of all people are equal, whether they live on the high mountains or at the bottoms of the valleys."
(*Tenrikyo,* Ofudesaki XIII 43–45)

"So what of all these titles, names, and races? They are mere worldly conventions."
(*Sutta Nipata* 648)

"No difference or preference has been made by God for its human inhabitants; but man has laid the foundation of prejudice, hatred and discord with his fellowman by considering nationalities separate in importance and races different in rights and privileges."
(*Bahá'í Faith,* Promulgation of Universal Peace, p. 232)

"Don't create enmity with anyone as God is within everyone."

(*Sikhism*, Guru Arjan Devji 259)

"Bahá'u'lláh teaches that an equal standard of human rights must be recognized and adopted. In the estimation of God all men are equal."

(Abdu'l-Bahá)

Fundamental to the idea of justice is the idea of equality. In the context of this book, I like to think of it as *righteous* equality—in other words, equality based not on political ideology but on the vision of the world's faith traditions, as sampled above. When I talk about righteous equality, I usually identify three distinct tenets. First is the belief that no one human being (or one group of human beings) is innately superior to another. Second is the conviction that human beings of all races, nationalities, political and religious persuasions, and so on, are fundamentally more alike than they are different. Third is the realization that there are enough resources on our planet for *everyone* to achieve a healthy and fulfilling life—in other words, there is plenty to go around if we choose to share it.

Justice and righteous equality are intimately related. As I mentioned in the previous chapter, rock icon Bono gave the keynote address at the 2006 National Prayer Breakfast. He described the relationship between justice and equality as a friendship. In his speech, he told President George W. Bush and other world leaders: "It's annoying, but justice and equality are mates.... Justice always wants to hang out with equality. And equality is a real pain."[1]

Why is equality such a pain? Because establishing righteous equality on a systemic, long-term basis is hard work. In chapter 5 we explored how giving as charity helps reduce some of the gap between those who have and those who have not by meeting immediate needs. But truly working for righteous equality and justice means understanding and solving the *causes* of hunger, the *causes* of homelessness, the *causes* of illiteracy. Justice challenges systemic issues such as economic structures, political powers, racial prejudices, and other entrenched ways of the world that perpetuate situations of inequality.

Although anyone can work for justice, and a lifestyle of generosity will most likely contain some measure of giving as justice, I happen to believe it is the responsibility of the powerful, the wealthy, and the privileged to take the lead in gifts of justice. But aspiring to the principles of righteous equality is more than an obligation. Those of us able to use our money to work for justice are also the recipients of a remarkable gift: we have the opportunity to be catalysts of actual change in the world. As Gloria Steinem, a key figure in the struggle for equality of women, observed, "It's more rewarding to watch money change the world than to watch it accumulate." Giving as justice has the potential to change the course of human history because when we practice justice giving we have the chance to tap into the sacred undercurrents running through the world. We get to acknowledge where the supernatural is actively working in the world for righteous equality and to orient ourselves toward this sacred purpose. We get to be about the work of God!

Money's Role in Freedom, Choice, and Power

One of the keys to understanding how money can effectively bring about justice when we *give* it, is first to understand some of the things that money does for us when we *keep* it. It's easy to imagine all the material things money can buy—cars, boats, jewelry. But are there any intangible things that money can bring us? Yes. Money is more than just a medium of exchange—it is worth more than its measure of value. I like to think that money offers us three things: money offers *freedom*; money offers *choice*;

money offers *power*. These three are closely related, but are distinct enough to warrant a separate discussion of each.

Money offers freedom by allowing us to not be controlled or restrained by our day-to-day needs or desires. For example, when we have money, our lives are not consumed with having to find a new way to feed ourselves every day. With money, we are also likely not obligated to work second and third jobs to support our families; instead, we have leisure time that we are free to spend with our families or however else we choose. With enough money we even have the freedom to pay someone else to do jobs we don't want to do, such as lawn care, housework, driving.

Money offers choice by allowing us to pick from a variety of options in most areas of life, from the simple and everyday to the life-altering and profound. For example, having money means we have options when it comes to what we wear each day, and having money can allow us choice in terms of which doctor we see, and when. Money even gives us the ability to choose the kind of lives we will lead. For example, an education at a good university opens up a lifetime of opportunities that you aren't likely to have if you can't afford college.

Money offers power by giving those who possess it control over how they live, and even control over how others live. For example, recently in Las Vegas I watched a high roller walk right past the queue formed for a fancy restaurant, slip the maître d' a hundred-dollar bill, and immediately sit down at the nicest table. With enough money, we have the power to choose our neighbors and control our contact with others by living in a gated community. Money also allows us to donate to political organizations, thereby exerting influence over our government with more than just our vote.

And we wield power via our money in other ways. When my husband and I picked out a car, we chose to purchase a hybrid vehicle despite its slightly higher cost, in order to support environmental health. This, in turn, exerted some influence over the car manufacturing industry and the decisions it makes with regard to making more hybrid vehicles. When we give to the local food bank, we are "voting" that the needy matter by contributing directly to the health of our community. On the other hand, when we purchase tabloid magazines, we are empowering the media machine that feeds on celebrity worship and paparazzi frenzy. We, as customers, have a lot of power. As Henry Ford aptly described, "It's not the employer who pays the wages. Employers only handle the money. It's the consumer who pays the wages."

When we keep money, it offers us freedom, choice, and power. On the flip side, when we give money, it offers the *recipient* freedom, choice, and power. Giving as justice is more than just sharing a certain monetary amount; it's about sharing energy and potential with groups that have been disenfranchised. It is establishing a righteous equality so that all people have access to the same life-giving energy sources. When you share goods and wealth, you also share freedom, choice, and power.

The word *share* may not be the most accurate way to describe what is happening with justice giving. What we are actually doing is *transferring* power. When we give, we give away some of the power that money and possessions afford us and transfer it to another group of people who deserve the same access to freedom, choice, and power. We as humans have a habit of categorizing people with simplistic labels and making judgments about who deserves what. But when you live by the tenet of righteous equality—that no one is better than another, that we are more alike than different, that everyone can experience a healthy, fulfilling life—you approach life differently. Through acts of justice you can transfer power to groups who need it and give life back to people who were once deemed only outcasts.

Because justice giving is about more than transferring money, you can be encouraged that no matter how much money you are able to contribute your gift will make a difference. In my seminars, someone often raises a concern that goes something like this: "What good will my thousand dollars do in the face of global hunger?" A more nuanced corollary is this: "If my thousand dollars goes to an organization, I never really see the effect it has for the real people who need it." These are legitimate concerns, but giving as justice has answers for these worries. My response is usually to counsel people to shift their perspective and stop thinking of their gift as merely cash and instead to think of it in terms of the freedom, choice, and power that accompany their money. In this way, you can begin to envision the effect your gift will have, even if it is mediated by an agency or organization, and even if you don't see identifiable, concrete results immediately.

By giving away, say, a thousand dollars, you may have lost the freedom to stay in a fancy hotel on your next trip out of town, but the organization you gave to now has the freedom to expand their programming to meet the needs of the community. You may have lost the choice of whether to buy tickets to the football game or watch it on television at home, but the organization now has the choice of whether or not to stay open an extra hour based on their needs. And you may have lost the power to attract attention with a fancy watch, but the organization has gained the power to lobby its agenda before influential politicians for another day.

The question, really, is not *whether* your thousand dollars is going to make a difference, as it is always going to make a difference. The question is, *where* it is going to make a difference. Will your money do its work in your own pocket by enriching your lifestyle? Or are you willing to give it away so it can exert its influence in another arena, where it can help others?

There is no doubt that giving money for justice is something of a sacrifice whether you give ten, a thousand, or ten thousand dollars. But transferring that money along with the freedom, choice, and power that it brings, in turn opens a door for you to tap into another, deeper energy source—a sacred power—that is working toward righteous equality throughout every moment of humanity's existence. No other kind of giving offers the chance to connect with such a potent force for good. You have the opportunity to identify and participate in the work of God. I would argue, therefore, that no other form of giving is as satisfying as justice giving.

With these things in mind, let's turn to some real-life examples. You will see how these specific acts of justice were set in motion by the desire for righteous equality. And looking at these cases may stir your imagination as to how you might begin to practice giving as justice. We will first look at an international medical mission group providing health care for underprivileged populations, and then examine a huge worldwide movement attempting to make poverty history. Finally, you will be given a number of basic ways to practice justice giving today that can contribute to creating a lifestyle of generosity.

RAM: HEALTH AND HOPE

One of the most effective and exciting organizations I have seen working for righteous equality is Remote Area Medical, or RAM. Founded by Stan Brock initially to provide medical care to remote parts of the world, this charity has now expanded its services to include the U.S. RAM holds giant medical clinics for uninsured or underinsured patients who drive from hundreds of miles away and line up hours in advance in hopes of receiving care from one of the more than 250 volunteer doctors and nurses. In 2007, RAM saw 17,000 patients.

The volunteers give their time and the donors give their money to RAM because they see that RAM's mission is to work for righteous equality—that is, they respect the patients (they believe they are no better than the people RAM serves); they see them as fellow human beings (they believe they have more in common than not with RAM patients); and they are generous with their resources (they believe there are enough resources on the planet for everyone to have a shot at good health). As a direct result of this giving, entire communities are given free checkups, dental care, glasses, and other forms of basic care that they would otherwise go without. Besides these essential health services, RAM also provides its patients with less concrete, but equally important, advantages, such as confidence in their appearance when they receive proper dental care.[2] It gives people the power to say, "I am worthy of care just as much as anyone else." RAM gives those on the outskirts of society health and hope, two things everyone is due.

JUBILEE 2000: RESTORING JUSTICE

A larger-scale example of justice giving is Jubilee 2000, an international movement to cancel third-world debt. The idea of Jubilee comes from the biblical notion in Leviticus that every fifty years debts are erased, land that was seized is returned, and justice is restored. By the year 2000, the movement had a petition signed by almost 20 million people in over 150 countries.[3] It also helped 27 countries to qualify for debt cancellation totaling 45 billion dollars by 2004.[4] Jubilee 2000 also gave birth to several offshoot organizations that continue its mission today. One of these groups is the Jubilee Debt Campaign in the United Kingdom. According to the organization's website, so far "more than 20 of the poorest countries in the world have received over 83 billion dollars in debt cancellation."[5]

Perhaps the most high-profile offshoot organization is the ONE campaign, made popular by numerous celebrity endorsements. The goal of this movement is to lobby the U.S. Congress to increase humanitarian aid by 1 percent in the federal budget. (The United States ranks last among industrialized countries in foreign aid as a percentage of gross national product. The United States gave 0.17 percent in 2006.) More specifically, the goal of the ONE campaign is to fight AIDS and extreme poverty in the world. Once again, the desire for righteous equality (the belief that everyone can experience a good life) has inspired justice (the act of giving others what is their due, in this case the chance at a good life). According to the campaign, a 1 percent increase would reduce by half the number of people in the world who suffer from hunger, provide free access to primary education for 77 million out-of-school children, provide access to clean water to 450 million people and basic sanitation to 700 million people, prevent 5.4 million young children from dying of poverty-related illnesses each year, and save 16,000 lives a day by fighting HIV/AIDS, Tuberculosis and Malaria.[6] All that—just by reallocating 1 percent of the U.S. budget. That 1 percent would not only shift money to "the least of these" in our world, it would transfer freedom, choice, and power to those who do not have it.

IT'S YOUR TURN

Remote Area Medical and Jubilee 2000 are just two examples of justice occurring in our world. You probably are familiar with several other charities or organizations working toward the tenets of righteous equality that motivate acts of justice. Underneath all of these *human* acts of justice is a metaphysical orientation toward the same goal. God is at work in the very fabric of creation to establish righteous equality through acts of justice. RAM and Jubilee 2000 are two examples of humanity tapping into these sacred undercurrents, sharing in its remarkable power, and participating in holy work. It is no wonder that people who give as an act of justice are very fulfilled; working alongside the Sacred certainly gives meaning to what you do. You too can access this supernatural energy. "One person, one voice, one vote at a time—to make a better, safer world for all." That's the motto for the ONE campaign. Creating justice may be about meeting the needs of groups of people, but it starts with the work of an individual. Here are a few things you could do:

- What groups of people are you most tempted to dis-
  criminate against: pregnant teens, illegal immigrants,
  smokers? Consider donating money to an organization
  that supports these people (not necessarily their actions)
  as a way to affirm their place in humanity.
- If you are a person of significant wealth, consider starting a donor-advised fund or a family foundation to
  benefit an issue of justice. These are long-term financial
  commitments and can be a great vehicle for enhancing
  a lifestyle of generosity. Be creative. Peter Norton made
  money in computer software and buys socially conscious art to support new artists. He then gives it away
  to museums. Most notably, he bought J. D. Salinger's
  letters to a young lover and then returned them to
  Salinger.
- Set up a scholarship fund at your alma mater or a local
  university, and give educational access to someone on
  "the outside." Scholarship funds do not have to be
  huge; keep in mind you don't have to pay for a student's entire tuition. A thousand dollars can go a
  long way.
- Add your name to the people standing as one at
  www.one.org. Use the power of your name to show
  support for the powerless.
- Buy products that are labeled "fair trade," such as
  certain brands of coffee, tea, and chocolate. Buying
  fair trade means you are paying enough for the product to ensure that the farmers and farm workers
  in developing countries can earn a living wage. Your
  purchase gives these working poor access to fair compensation and the freedoms of life that come with a
  just salary.
- Be aware of what is going on in the world through a
  variety of media outlets. You will learn the stories of

the marginalized from more than one perspective and can then be a voice for the voiceless. When you are well informed, people will listen when you speak, particularly when you are part of a majority speaking on behalf of a minority.

- Use your presence to draw attention to injustice. Just showing up in support of the oppressed is a huge gift. Attend protests or rallies to unite with fellow human beings against issues or acts of injustice. The more bodies that are gathered, the more attention the issue is going to get.

- Speak up. There are hundreds of classifications of "the other" that are easily stereotyped and discriminated against: the mentally ill, gays and lesbians, the obese. When you hear stereotypes being perpetuated, say something. The next time you hear an irreverent joke about a certain type of person, don't laugh. Better yet, respond with a polite but firm explanation of why that stereotype is incorrect. When someone forwards you an offensive e-mail, write back and explain why you don't find that depiction of the person or group accurate.

- Practice tonglen, a Tibetan Buddhist practice of giving and receiving, or sending and taking. Tonglen is a way to awaken compassion and connect with those around us who are suffering. To practice, sit quietly and breathe in the suffering and pain of others. Breathe out joy and peace and send it to those in need. For example, if you know of a family that is grieving a death, breathe in their sorrow and hurt. For a moment, take on their emotional burden by momentarily experiencing it for them. Then, breathing out, send them hope that tomorrow will be better than today.

- Be a voice of accountability for media. The communications industry has tremendous power when it comes to shaping how we view "the other." Write letters to the newspaper when the marginalized are being overlooked. Call the local television station when a group is being portrayed unfairly. By doing so, you are helping to redistribute power away from the giants and back into the hands of the little guys.

- If you have a public voice, use it to depict marginalized people in a positive light. Politicians, clergy, teachers, and anyone else who "speaks to the masses" can provide civic conversation that more equitably shifts the tide of goodwill toward minority groups.

- Before you vote for an elected official, take time to learn about each candidate's history on public policy. Think about your needs and the needs of "the other." Which nominee do you think will give the entire breadth of humanity access to basic human rights?

- Have a party! Get together a bunch of your friends (particularly the kind who like to make things happen) and a representative from a nonprofit. The goal of the session is not for the friends to give money directly to the nonprofit (save that for the annual gala). Instead, the nonprofit rep can come with a list of needs, and the group of movers-and-shakers can use their social capital (and their ever-present cell phones) to make a few connections and see what they can have donated right then and there. On the list might be office supplies, the services of a lawyer, an event planner for the golf fund-raiser, a consultant to give advice about marketing. Sure, nonprofits have boards, but anyone who has served on a board knows they can only do so much. The most exciting example I've seen of this type of make-it-happen party is a room full of corporate men and women who come together once a month on their lunch break. All they bring is their cell phone (no wallets), and within an hour a nonprofit representative walks away with a dozen needs met. These corporate men and women transfer their power (their power to talk to important people, their power to ask favors, their power to get things for free) to the nonprofit sector so that nonprofits can (momentarily) have access to the same resources as corporations.

How Justice Changes the World

Hopefully you have identified a few ways to start your justice giving. However you choose to live out "giving others what is their due" will offer you the chance to change the world. But *how* exactly? We've already talked about justice as an opportunity for us to partner with God in doing work for the world, work fueled by a blessed energy source. But what are some of the actual mechanisms of change? What are some of the characteristic goals that mark the sacred undercurrents we can tap into and orient ourselves toward through justice-giving? I have identified four: peace, reconciliation, future generations, and repairing the world.

Giving for Peace

Did you ever consider giving as a way toward peace? In our world we are often conditioned to think that peace is best achieved and maintained by force or threat of arms, but there are limits to what military power can achieve. When we give as justice, we speak into those limitations and acknowledge hope in something greater than weapons. Dave Toycen, President and CEO of World Vision Canada, writes "Perhaps the greatest challenge to finding peace in the midst of conflict is the demand to look beyond the immediate situation.... Generosity increases our ability to see what is not readily apparent."[7] People who have been dealt an injustice (or even those who *feel* that way) often are marginalized and act out violently because it is the only way for their voice to be heard. The "haves" then have a choice how to react. Reacting with force is one option, but responding with giving allows the "have-nots" to have their needs met and not feel their only option is to cry out through fighting. The Dalai Lama said, "If you wish to experience peace, provide peace for another." And from Judaism we read: "The more *tzedakah* (righteous giving), the more shalom (peace)" (Talmud *Pirke Avot* 2:8). When we give to groups of people who are owed something, rather than turning to military force, we give them hope—hope that there is a God who daily orients the fabric of life toward righteous equality.

GIVING FOR RECONCILIATION

Justice giving also changes the world by allowing reconciliation to occur. Oppressed communities typically become isolated from mainstream society, but justice giving allows them to reconnect. In Indianapolis, for example, an organization called Rebuilding the Wall is leading the way toward righteous equality. This nonprofit works to "stabilize and empower low-income families by renovating vacant inner-city properties and giving the families the opportunity for homeownership." In short, inner-city homes are refurbished and families who otherwise couldn't afford it get the chance to live in a safe and secure environment. Rebuilding the Wall understands their work as part of a larger righteous-equality-related movement. Their mission statement further says, "We combat social injustice by building relationships across racial and socioeconomic barriers." In other words, they see the potential in their giving as far more than four walls and a roof. They partner urban families with small groups, and the combined teams work for two years toward achieving home ownership for the family. Along the way, the group forms a relationship that crosses racial and socioeconomic lines. The people at Rebuilding the Wall are changing their corner of the world one family at a time.

GIVING FOR FUTURE GENERATIONS

A third way that justice goes about changing the world is by providing for future generations. One of the strongest links between past, current, and future generations is the holy undercurrent running throughout all of time and space that orients the universe toward the tenets of righteous equality (we are all valuable as humans; we are more alike than we think; there's space on the planet for everyone to be fulfilled). But a word of warning: justice giving provides long-lasting change, but it requires a great deal of patience. Changing power structures, addressing deeply entrenched historical and cultural beliefs, and swaying public opinion takes a long time and may not reach its full fruition in your lifetime. This is one of the reasons that giving as justice is arguably the most difficult form of giving. Consider issues like slavery, women's suffrage, segregation; these took generations to work through, and the work continues today.

GIVING FOR REPAIRING THE WORLD

A final example of how justice giving can transform our world is by repairing it in areas where it is broken. Jewish tradition calls this *tikkun olam*, a Hebrew phrase that literally means "to mend or repair the world." This Jewish practice reflects the belief that while God created a good world, things go awry, so the world is in constant need of mending. You are invited to join with the Creator and restore the beliefs of righteous equality through acts of justice giving. By doing so, you are repairing the world. You'll remember Alan Slifka, cofounder of the Abraham Fund. He says, "Doing philanthropy is the reason I exist. Why work if not to make money to help other people. I believe in *tikkun olam* … that we are put on this Earth to repair the Earth!"[8]

ONE STEP AT A TIME

You are now equipped with an entire tool-kit of resources to begin your journey into the sacred art of giving. With these tools you have the chance to become more like God, to shape your identity into one of instinctive generosity, to form deep relationships with all walks of humanity, and to change the world.

> "The Buddha said, 'When you see someone practicing the Way of giving, aid him joyously, and you will obtain vast and great blessings.' A shramana asked: 'Is there an end to those blessings?' The Buddha said, 'Consider the flame of a single lamp. Though a hundred thousand people come and light their own lamps from it so that they can cook their food and ward off the darkness, the first lamp remains the same as before. Blessings are like this, too.'"
>
> (*Tripitaka Sutra* 10)

The possibilities of giving are endless. You are invited to create a *lifestyle* of generosity, so think about steady and sustainable ways to practice giving. We can't all go out and open a school in Africa for young girls, but we can all do something. Take it from Mother Teresa, "If you can't feed a hundred people, just feed one." Whatever you do, may it be done with a generous spirit for the sake of God and your fellow human beings. Amen.

> "They who give have all things; they who withhold have nothing."
>
> —(Hindu Proverb)

A P P E N D I C E S

TO DETERMINE YOUR "EXTRA-ABUNDANCE"...

Determine the amount of money coming in each year (Appendix A).

Determine the amount of money going out each year (Appendix B).

Subtract expenses from income (Appendix C).

USING THIS KNOWLEDGE...

Create a budget for the future (Appendix D).

It is the suggestion of the author that you do these exercises using the numbers reflective of your entire household. However, it is still possible to limit the exercises to your saving and spending habits.

Photocopy appendices before entering information, so that you can reuse the worksheets as your financial situation changes.

You can also visit http://www.laurentylerwright.org to download a copy.

APPENDIX A

HOW MUCH MONEY DO I RECEIVE EACH YEAR?

_____ Gross Wages (after all deductions like taxes and Social Security)

_____ Retirement (IRA, 401k, Pension)

_____ Social Security

_____ Interest/Dividends (Savings Accounts, Money Market Accounts, Mutual Funds, Stocks and Bonds)

_____ Annuities

_____ Certificates of Deposit (CDs)

_____ Rental Income

_____ Child Support/Alimony Received

_____ Tax Refunds

_____ Other Income

Add the numbers above to compute your total

_____ TOTAL Amount of Money I Receive Each Year

If you want some point of comparison, consider looking at your Adjusted Gross Income (AGI). It is the last number on the first page of the tax Form 1040, the standard U.S. income tax return form for individuals. Hopefully, the AGI and the number you have determined here are somewhat similar.

This material is from *Giving—The Sacred Art* by Lauren Tyler Wright © 2008, published by SkyLight Paths Publishing, P.O. Box 237, Woodstock, VT 05091. (802) 457-4000; www.skylightpaths.com. The Publisher grants permission to you to copy this handout. All rights to other parts of this book are still covered by copyright and are reserved to the Publisher. Any other copying or usage requires written permission.

A P P E N D I X   B

H O W   M U C H   M O N E Y   D O   I   S P E N D   E A C H   Y E A R ?

Home

_____ Mortgage or Rent

_____ Electricity

_____ Gas

_____ Water

_____ Sewer

_____ Garbage

_____ Recycling

_____ Property Tax

_____ Phone (landline)

_____ Maintenance

_____ Homeowners/Rent Insurance

_____ Furnishings

_____ Other Home _____

TOTAL Home Expenses _____

Food

_____ Groceries (non-food items included if typically purchased at grocery store)

_____ Fast Food/Take-Out/Delivery

_____ Restaurants/Table-Service

_____ Snacks/Coffee/Alcohol

_____ Other Food _____

TOTAL Food Expenses _____

This material is from *Giving—The Sacred Art* by Lauren Tyler Wright © 2008, published by SkyLight Paths Publishing, P.O. Box 237, Woodstock, VT 05091. (802) 457-4000; www.skylightpaths.com. The Publisher grants permission to you to copy this handout. All rights to other parts of this book are still covered by copyright and are reserved to the Publisher. Any other copying or usage requires written permission.

Recreation

_____ Vacation

_____ Entertainment (movies, sporting events)

_____ Cable

_____ Internet

_____ Cell Phones

_____ Hobbies/Personal Interests

_____ Subscription/Membership and Dues

_____ Cigarettes

_____ Other Recreation _____

TOTAL Recreation Expenses _____

Personal Care

_____ Clothes/Shoes

_____ Alterations

_____ Toiletries/Cosmetics

_____ Dry Cleaning/Laundry

_____ Hair Cuts/Color

_____ Other Personal Care _____

TOTAL Personal Care Expenses _____

Transportation

_____ Car Payment/Lease

_____ Gas

_____ Insurance

_____ Tax, Title, Registration, Tags, License

_____ Maintenance

_____ Public Transportation

_____ Other Transportation _____

TOTAL Transportation Expenses _____

This material is from *Giving—The Sacred Art* by Lauren Tyler Wright © 2008, published by SkyLight Paths Publishing, P.O. Box 237, Woodstock, VT 05091. (802) 457-4000; www.skylightpaths.com. The Publisher grants permission to you to copy this handout. All rights to other parts of this book are still covered by copyright and are reserved to the Publisher. Any other copying or usage requires written permission.

Health Care

_____ Health Insurance Premium

_____ Health Insurance Out-of-pocket Deductible

_____ Health Insurance Co-pays

_____ Dental and Vision Insurance

_____ Prescriptions

_____ Over-the-counter Medications

_____ Uninsured or Not-covered Expenses

_____ Mental Health Care (counselor, psychiatrist)

_____ Health Club Membership

_____ Other Health Care _____

TOTAL Health Care Expenses _____

Debts

_____ Credit Card

_____ College Loans

_____ Bank Loans

_____ Loans from Individuals

_____ Other Debts _____

TOTAL Debts Expenses _____

Children

_____ Day Care

_____ Preschool

_____ Baby-sitting

_____ Child Support

_____ Allowances

_____ Private School

_____ Other Children _____

TOTAL Children Expenses _____

This material is from *Giving—The Sacred Art* by Lauren Tyler Wright © 2008, published by SkyLight Paths Publishing, P.O. Box 237, Woodstock, VT 05091. (802) 457-4000; www.skylightpaths.com. The Publisher grants permission to you to copy this handout. All rights to other parts of this book are still covered by copyright and are reserved to the Publisher. Any other copying or usage requires written permission.

Pets

_____ Adopting Animal

_____ Food

_____ Veterinarian Care

_____ Toys and Treats

_____ Grooming

_____ Boarding

_____ Other Pet _____

TOTAL Pets Expenses _____

Aging Parent

_____ Home Health Nurse

_____ Assisted Living Facility/Nursing Home

_____ Expenses he/she can no longer cover

_____ Other Aging Parent _____

TOTAL Aging Parent Expenses _____

Savings

_____ Deposits to a Savings Account

_____ Deposits to a Retirement Fund (IRA/401k)

_____ Purchase of Stocks/Bonds/Mutual Funds/CDs/ Money Market Funds/Annuities

_____ Deposits to a College Fund for Children or Grandchildren

_____ Emergency Fund

_____ Other Savings _____

TOTAL Savings Expenses _____

This material is from *Giving—The Sacred Art* by Lauren Tyler Wright © 2008, published by SkyLight Paths Publishing, P.O. Box 237, Woodstock, VT 05091. (802) 457-4000; www.skylightpaths.com. The Publisher grants permission to you to copy this handout. All rights to other parts of this book are still covered by copyright and are reserved to the Publisher. Any other copying or usage requires written permission.

Gifts

_____ Faith Community
_____ Charitable Organization
_____ Holiday Giving
_____ Birthday/Anniversary Presents
_____ Other Gifts _____

TOTAL Gifts Expenses _____

Other

_____ _____

_____ _____

_____ _____

TOTAL Other Expenses _____

Add the above subtotals to compute your total

TOTAL ANNUAL EXPENSES _____

Keep in mind, the most accurate way to achieve this figure is by keeping receipts of everything you purchase for at least a month. Then record those purchases in a chart like this, so you are sure you're not missing purchases. If you record purchases for a month, multiply each category by twelve. If you feel that one or more of the categories does not reflect the traditional spending practices of your family, adjust as necessary.

This material is from *Giving—The Sacred Art* by Lauren Tyler Wright © 2008, published by SkyLight Paths Publishing, P.O. Box 237, Woodstock, VT 05091. (802) 457-4000; www.skylightpaths.com. The Publisher grants permission to you to copy this handout. All rights to other parts of this book are still covered by copyright and are reserved to the Publisher. Any other copying or usage requires written permission.

APPENDIX C

WHAT'S LEFT? DEBT OR EXTRA-ABUNDANCE?

Enter the total from Appendix A here: _____
(income)

Enter the total from Appendix B here: _____
(expenses)

If the top line is larger than the bottom line, your difference is one of extra-abundance.

If the bottom line is larger than the top line, your difference is one of debt.

Subtract the bottom line from the top line and note the difference: _____

I, _____ , as of _____
(name)   *(date)*

have _____ in _____ . This
(difference between income and expense)   *(debt or extra-abundance)*

news makes me feel _____ .

This material is from *Giving—The Sacred Art* by Lauren Tyler Wright © 2008, published by SkyLight Paths Publishing, P.O. Box 237, Woodstock, VT 05091. (802) 457-4000; www.skylightpaths.com. The Publisher grants permission to you to copy this handout. All rights to other parts of this book are still covered by copyright and are reserved to the Publisher. Any other copying or usage requires written permission.

APPENDIX D

CREATING A BUDGET

Using what you've learned about your earning, saving, and spending habits in the first three appendices, you can now effectively create a budget in this final appendix. Below, enter numbers that you want to see happen in the future. Based on what you know from the past exercises, you can make realistic expectations. But don't be afraid to dream big.

Expected Income	Expected Expenses	Expected Extra-Abundance
_____ Gross Wages (after all deductions like taxes and Social Security)	_____ Home	_____ Faith Community
_____ Retirement (IRA, 401k, Pension)	_____ Food	_____ Charitable Organization
_____ Social Security	_____ Recreation	_____ Individuals
_____ Interest/ Dividends (Savings Accounts, Money Market Accounts, Mutual Funds, Stocks and Bonds)	_____ Personal Care	_____ Other
	_____ Transportation	
	_____ Health Care	
	_____ Debts	
	_____ Children	
_____ Annuities	_____ Pets	
_____ Certificates of Deposit (CDs)	_____ Aging Parent	
_____ Rental Income	_____ Savings	
_____ Child Support/ Alimony Received	_____ Other	
_____ Tax Refunds	*See appendix B for more details re categories.*	
_____ Other Income		
Total Income (a) = _____	Total Expenses (b) = _____	Total Extra (c) = _____

1. Total Extra (c) _____ X 100 = _____ (d).
2. _____ (d) / Total Income (a) _____ = _____ (e)
3. (e) _____ = % of your total income you give away

This material is from *Giving—The Sacred Art* by Lauren Tyler Wright © 2008, published by SkyLight Paths Publishing, P.O. Box 237, Woodstock, VT 05091. (802) 457-4000; www.skylightpaths.com. The Publisher grants permission to you to copy this handout. All rights to other parts of this book are still covered by copyright and are reserved to the Publisher. Any other copying or usage requires written permission.

N O T E S

INTRODUCTION

1. The following research affirms that religious people are among the most generous in the world:

> "Of givers to religious congregations, over 85 percent also support secular organizations, providing three-quarters of the philanthropic support those other organizations receive.... Fifty-four percent of those who regularly attend religious services volunteer, while only 32 percent of the non-attendees volunteer."
>
> —Independent Sector, "Faith and Philanthropy: The Connection Between Charitable Behavior and Giving to Religion," *Giving & Volunteering in the United States Signature Series* (Washington: The Independent Sector, 2002), 9.

> "Religious people are 25 percentage points more likely than secularists to donate money (91 percent to 66 percent) and 23 points more likely to volunteer time (67 percent to 44 percent).... The average annual giving among the religious is $2,210, whereas it is $642 among the secular.... Religious people volunteer an average of 12 times per year, while secular people volunteer an average of 5.8 times.... Religious people are 33 percent of the population

but make 52 percent of donations and 45 percent of times volunteered. Secular people are 26 percent of the population but contribute 13 percent of the dollars and 17 percent of the times volunteered.... Religious practice by itself is associated with $1,388 more given per year than we would expect to see from a secular person (with the same political views, income, education, age, race, and other characteristics), as well as with 6.5 more occasions of volunteering."

—Arthur C. Brooks, "Religious Faith and Charitable Giving," *Policy Review* 121 (October/November 2003).

2. Religion is by far the largest recipient of all charitable contributions, surpassing education, health, human services, arts, public society benefit, environment/animals, international affairs, and gifts to foundations. Brown, Melissa S., ed., *Giving USA 2006: The Annual Report on Philanthropy for the Year 2005* (Glenview: Giving USA Foundation, 2006), 16.

3. Giving of the human body is one of the few exceptions where people of faith are not the most generous. "People who have given money to religious charities are no more or no less likely to have given blood in the previous year than other people, but they are much less likely to be willing to donate organs or their whole body to science"—IU Center for Bioethics at IUPUI "Health Related Philanthropy: The Donation of the Body (and Parts Thereof)," from *Final Report of the Health-Related Philanthropy Study Group*, (Indianapolis: IU Center for Bioethics at IUPUI December 2004).

4. Wuthnow, Robert, *Acts of Compassion: Caring for Others and Helping Ourselves* (Princeton: Princeton University Press, 1991), 88.

CHAPTER ONE

1. Gay, Craig, *Cash Values: Money and the Erosion of Meaning in Today's Society* (Grand Rapids: W. B. Eerdmans, 2004), 91–4.

2. *Alcoholics Anonymous* (New York: Alcoholics Anonymous World Services, Inc., 2001), 59.

3. Gomes, Peter, *The Good Book*. (New York: William Morrow, 1996), 287.

4. *Merriam-Webster Online Dictionary* s.v. "worship." http://www. m-w.com (accessed May 15, 2008).

5. Vincent, Mark, *A Christian View of Money: Celebrating God's Generosity* (Scottsdale: Herald Press, 1997), 22–3.

6. Simmel, Georg. *The Philosophy of Money*, 2nd ed., (London: Routledge, 1990), 236.

CHAPTER TWO

1. How, William W., "We Give Thee but Thine Own," 1864.

2. Carnegie, Andrew, *The Gospel of Wealth,* Essays on Philanthropy Series (Indianapolis: Indiana University Center on Philanthropy, 1993), 8.

3. "18,000 Children Die Every Day of Hunger, U.N. Says," *USA Today*, February 17, 2007. http://www.usatoday.com/news/world/ 2007-02-17-un-hunger_x.htm.

4. Christian Reformed World Relief Committee "Food Distribution Around the World: How Much Food Do You Get to Eat?" http://www.crcna.org/site_uploads/uploads/crwrc_ff_ fooddistribution.pdf.

5. Wallis, Jim, *God's Politics: Why the Right Gets it Wrong and the Left Doesn't Get it* (New York: Harper Collins, 2005), 241.

6. Payton, Robert L., and Michael Moody, "Stewardship," in *Philanthropy in America: A Comprehensive Historical Encyclopedia*, ed. by Dwight F. Burlingame (Santa Barbara: ABC-CLIO, 2004), 457–60.

7. Frumkin, Peter, *Strategic Giving: The Art and Science of Philanthropy.* (Chicago: University of Chicago Press, 2006), 125.

8. National Center for Charitable Statistics/Center on Nonprofits and Philanthropy and the Center on Philanthropy at Indiana University, *Nonprofit Overhead Cost Study* (Indianapolis: The Urban Institute and Indiana University, 2004) 3, http://www. coststudy.org.

9. Willmer, Wesley Kenneth, *God and Your Stuff: The Vital Link between Your Possessions and Your Soul* (Colorado Springs: NavPress, 2002), 95.

10. Berry, Wendell, as quoted in *Having: Property and Possession in Religious and Social Life*, Matthewes, Charles T., and William Schweiker eds. (Grand Rapids: Wm. B. Eerdmans Publishing. 2004), 212.

11. Gard, Lauren, "Ordinary People, Extraordinary Gifts," *Business Week* (November 29, 2004), 94. http://www.albertlexie.org

12. Adlerstein, Rabbi Yizchok, "Let the Giver Beware" *Jewish Action* Winter 5760 (1999), http://www.ou.org/publications/ja/5760 winter/bytes&pcs.pdf.

CHAPTER THREE

1. Stein, Joseph, *Fiddler on the Roof* (director's script, New York: Sunbeam Music Corp, 1964), 1-P-3.

2. Chaim, Chafetz, *Ahavath Chesed: The Love of Kindness As Required by God, 2nd ed.* (New York: Feldheim, 1976). 171.

3. Brown, Melissa S., ed. *Giving USA 2006: The Annual Report on Philanthropy for the Year 2005* (Glenview: Giving USA Foundation, 2006), 38.

4. Hart, Stephen, *General Social Survey 1987–1989* (Davis and Smith, 1994); data used in Mark Chaves and Sharon L. Miller, eds., *Financing American Religion* (Walnut Creek: AltaMira, 1999), 5.

5. Vivekananda, Swami, "We Help Ourselves, Not the World," *Karma-Yoga* in vol. 1 of *The Complete Works of Swami Vivekananda* (Chicago, 1893), http://www.ramakrishnavivekananda.info/ vivekananda/volume_1/vol_1_frame.htm.

6. Hauerwas, Stanley, with John Berkman, and Michael Cartwright, eds., *The Hauerwas Reader* (Durham: Duke University Press, 2001), 114.

7. The italicized text was excerpted from *Hilchot Matnot Ani'im, Laws on Gifts to the Poor* 10:7–14, appearing in a tractate called *Sefer Zera'im (Book of Seeds)*.

CHAPTER FOUR

1. Herper, Matthew, "Money Won't Buy You Happiness," *Forbes* (September 21, 2004). http://www.forbes.com/work/2004/09/21/ cx_mh_0921happiness.html.

2. Ellul, Jacques, *Money and Power* (Grand Rapids: Inter-Varsity Press, 1984), 196.

3. COPPS 2003. While 67.3 percent of Americans give at least $25, the average person who is philanthropic gives away $2,000 or 3 percent of their income. Secular people give away on average 1 percent; religious people give away 3 percent (2 percent to their faith community and 1 percent elsewhere), p. 69 of Giving USA 2006.

4. Crown Financial Ministries, Small Group Financial Study (1986), 37.
5. Kadlec, Daniel, "Get Out of Hock," *Time* (May 22, 2000).
6. Slifka, Alan, as quoted by Deanne Stone in "Alan B. Slifka: One Man's Faith-Based Mission," *National Center Journal: Faith and Family Philanthropy* Vol 4, (2001), 108.
7. Rockefeller, John D., 1905. http://archive.rockefeller.edu/bio/ jdrsr.php.
8. Wesley, John, "The Use of Money," Sermon 50 from the 1872 edition, Thomas Jackson, ed. The United Methodist Church Global Ministries, http://new.gbgm-umc.org/umhistory/wesley/sermons/50/

CHAPTER FIVE

1. Malins, Joseph, "The Ambulance Down in the Valley," 1895.
2. Benedict XVI, Pope, *Deus Caritas Est*, December 25, 2005.
3. Those who are oppressed by poverty are the object of a preferential love on the part of the Church which, since her origin and in spite of the failings of many of her members, has not ceased to work for their relief, defense and liberation through numerous works of charity which remain indispensable always and everywhere" (Catechism of the Catholic Church paragraph 2448). While Catholics are called to give to all (no one person is more deserving than another), the distribution of God's resources should be as equitable as possible. Therefore, preferential treatment is given to the poor.
4. References to caring for the poor from the Hebrew Bible:

   "And when you reap the harvest in your land, you shall not reap the corners of your field; neither shall you gather the gleaning of your harvest. And you shall not glean your vineyard, nor shall you gather the single grapes of your vineyard. You shall leave them for the poor and the stranger."

   —Leviticus 19:9–10

   "And when your brother will become poor and you will extend your hand to him."

   —Leviticus 25:35

"Share your bread with the hungry and make the wretched poor into your home: when you see the naked clothe them."

—Isaiah 58:7

"When you reap your harvest in your field, and you forget a sheaf in the field, you shall not go back to get it. It shall be for the stranger, the fatherless, and the widow; that the Lord your God will bless you in all the work of your hands."

—Deuteronomy 24:19–20

"If, however, there is a needy person among you ... do not harden your heart and shut your hand against your needy kinsman. Rather you must open your hand and lend him sufficient for whatever he needs."

—Deuteronomy 15:7–8

"The rich and poor meet together; God is the maker of them all."

—Proverbs 22:2

"He who is kind to the poor, happy is he."

—Proverbs 14:21

5. When a (poor) man says, "Provide me with clothes," he should be investigated (lest he be found to be a cheat); when he says, "Feed me," he should not be investigated but fed immediately, lest he starve to death during the investigation (Talmud *Baba Batra*).

   If a poor person who is a stranger says "I am hungry, feed me," we don't investigate whether he is a fraud but we sustain him immediately. If he were naked and said "clothe me," we investigate whether he is a fraud. But if we recognize him, we clothe him immediately in accordance with his position and we don't investigate him (Maimonides, *Mishneh Torah, Laws of Gifts to the Poor*, 87).

6. Carnegie, Andrew, *The Gospel of Wealth*, Essays on Philanthropy Series (Indianapolis: Indiana University Center on Philanthropy, 1993), 9.

CHAPTER SIX

1. Bono, "Keynote Address at the 54th National Prayer Breakfast" (Washington D.C., February 2, 2006), http://www.americanrhetoric.com/speeches/bononationalprayerbreakfast.htm.

2. "U.S. Health Care Gets Boost From Charity," *60 Minutes*, February 28, 2008, http://www.cbsnews.com/stories/2008/02/28/60minutes/main3889496.shtml.

3. Pettifor, Ann, *The World Will Never Be the Same Again* (Jubilee 2000 Coalition, December 2000), 17.

4. Nowels, Larry, *Debt Reduction: Initiatives for the Most Heavily Indebted Poor Countries* (U.S. Congress Congressional Research Service Report RL30214 February 1, 2000). http://www.ncseonline.org/nle/crsreports/international/inter-18.cfm, and Hornbeck, J. F., *Debt and Developing in Poor Countries: Rethinking Policy Responses* (U.S. Congress Congressional Research Report RL30449, March 1, 2000).

5. Jubilee Debt Campaign, "How Much Debt Has Been Cancelled?" http://www.jubileedebtcampaign.org.uk/?lid=3408.

6. One, "More and Better Aid," One: The Campaign to Make Poverty History http://www.one.org/issues/ (accessed June 3, 2008).

7. Toycen, Dave, *The Power of Generosity: How to Transform Yourself and the World* (Waynesboro: Authentic Media, 2004), 76.

8. Slifka, Alan, as quoted by Deanne Stone in "Alan B. Slifka: One Man's Faith-Based Mission," *National Center Journal: Faith and Family Philanthropy* Vol 4, (2001), 108.

GLOSSARY

al-Razzaq The name for God as ultimate provider (Islam).

al-Wahhab The name for God as ultimate giver (Islam).

charity Benevolent goodwill toward or love of humanity; generosity and helpfulness especially toward the needy or suffering; doing good for individuals who have immediate needs.

chesed Rendering mercies or kindnesses (Judaism).

diakonia Literally "service;" Practicing charity (Christianity).

extra-abundance Surplus of resources over and above the level needed to maintain a chosen lifestyle.

fair trade Social movement working to alleviate poverty and create a just and sustainable economy in the world; responsibly employs marginalized farmers and workers (for example, paying a living wage); issues a standard of "fair trade" for products like coffee, tea, or chocolate that meet the requirements of a certification system.

giving Voluntarily transferring something from one person to another without expecting compensation.

g'milut chasadim Acts of lovingkindness (Judaism).

imitation Dei The belief that it is good to imitate God (Judaism, Christianity).

justice The act or practice of giving to others what is their due; doing good for groups who are owed something.

kerygma-martyria Proclaiming the word of God (Christianity).

leitourgia Ministry or service of celebrating the sacraments (Christianity).

ma'aser The Hebrew word for tithing (Judaism).

ma'aser kesofim A tenth of income to use for charitable purposes (Judaism).

Maimonides' Ladder The oldest and most well-known hierarchy of giving levels; created by Moses Maimonides; eight levels of distributing *tzedakah* (Judaism).

mitzvah A duty or obligation to God (Judaism).

modus vivendi A lifestyle, a manner of living.

nisab A standard of eligible wealth. Those who exceed the standard are expected to give 2.5 percent of their wealth away to the poor (Islam).

obligation Something one is bound to do.

other Groups of individuals who are in the minority because of a particular characteristic; often marginalized and discriminated against because they are different.

prosperity gospel The belief that giving generously (as an act of faith) will earn material prosperity from God (Christianity).

pushke A container used to collect money for *tzedakah* (righteous giving); typically found in homes, synagogues, and schools (Judaism).

redeem To buy back; to free what distresses or harms; to change for the better.

righteous equality A set of beliefs fundamental to the practice of justice—the first belief: no one person is innately better than another; the second belief: humans are more alike than we are different; the third belief: there is room on the planet for everyone to experience a healthy and fulfilling life.

sadaqah Charity given voluntarily over and above the 2.5 percent minimum represented by *zakat* (alms tax) often given directly from giver to recipient; includes monetary and non-monetary giving (Islam).

salah Practicing prayer five times daily; one of the Five Pillars of Islam.

sawn Fasting, typically done during Ramadan; one of the Five Pillars of Islam.

stewardship The conducting, supervising, or managing of something— especially the careful and responsible management of something entrusted to one's care.

takhallaqu bi-akhlaqi llah The belief that it is good to take on the qualities of God (Islam).

tikkun olam Literally "mending" or "repairing" the world; modern Social Justice (Judaism).

tithe The practice of giving away 10 percent of your income; most often based on text from the Hebrew Bible.

tonglen A practice of giving and receiving (Buddhism).

tzedakah Righteous giving; combines the concepts of charity and justice (Judaism).

worship Reverence offered a divine being or supernatural power; an act of expressing such reverence.

zakat Obligatory alms tax; literally means "to grow in purity;" one of the Five Pillars of Islam; 2.5 percent of a person's wealth collected each year, typically during Ramadan, and distributed to the poor via a central authority (Islam).

SUGGESTIONS FOR FURTHER READING

My bookshelf is filled with an endless line of books on the intersection of faith, money, possessions, and giving. Some are good, some are not so good. Here are the ones I would recommend if you wish to continue reading on the subject. While I may not fully agree with everything these authors have to say, I find their writings a helpful addition to the discussion.

CHILDREN AND YOUTH

Roehlkepartain, Eugene C., Elanah Dalyah Naftali, and Laura Musegades. *Growing Up Generous: Engaging Youth in Giving and Serving.* Herndon: Alban Institute, 2000.

Sabin, Ellen. *The Giving Book: Open the Door to a Lifetime of Giving.* New York: Watering Can Press, 2004.

Silverstein, Shel. *The Giving Tree.* New York: HarperCollins, 2004.

FAITH-BASED GIVING

Alcorn, Randy. *Money, Possessions, and Eternity.* Wheaton: Tyndale House Publishers, 2003.

————. *The Treasure Principle: Unlocking the Secret of Joyful Giving.* Colorado Springs: Multnomah Books, 2005.

Brackett, John K. *On the Pilgrim's Way: Christian Stewardship and the Tithe.* Harrisburg: Morehouse Publishing, 1996.

Bush, Lawrence, and Jeffrey Dekro. *Jews, Money and Social Responsibility: Developing a "Torah of Money" for Contemporary Life.* Washington: B'nai B'rith Book Service, 1993.

Dorff, Elliot N. *The Way Into* Tikkun Olam *(Repairing the World)*. Woodstock: Jewish Lights Publishing, 2007.

Ellul, Jacques. *Money and Power*. Grand Rapids: Inter-Varsity Press, 1984.

Eskridge, Larry, and Mark A. Noll, eds. *More Money, More Minsitry: Money and Evangelicals in Recent North American History*. Grand Rapids: Wm. B. Eerdmans Publishing, 2000.

Gay, Craig M. *Cash Values: Money and the Erosion of Meaning in Today's Society*. Grand Rapids: Wm. B. Eerdmans Publishing, 2004.

Gomes, Peter. "The Bible and Wealth." In *The Good Book: Reading the Bible with Mind and Heart*. New York: HarperOne, 2002, 285-312.

Hales, Edward J., and J. Alan Youngren. *Your Money, Their Ministry: A Guide to Responsible Christian Giving*. Grand Rapids: Wm. B. Eerdmans Publishing, 1981.

Lupton, Robert. *And You Call Yourself a Christian: Toward Responsible Charity*. Chicago: Chicago Christian Community Development Association, 2006.

MacDonald, Gordon. *Secrets of the Generous Life: Reflections to Awaken the Spirit & Enrich the Soul*. Wheaton: Tyndale House, 2002.

McChesney, Robert D. "Charity and Philanthropy in Islam: Institutionalizing the Call to Do Good." *Essays on Philanthropy, 14* Indianapolis: Center on Philanthropy, 2007.

Miller, Lynn A. *The Power of Enough: Finding Contentment by Putting Stuff in Its Place*. Goshen: Stewardship Solutions, 2007.

Neusner, Jacob. *Tzedakah: Can Jewish Philanthropy Buy Jewish Survival?* New York: Union for Reform Judaism Press, 1997.

Oates, Mary J. *The Catholic Philanthropic Traditions in America*. Bloomington: Indiana University Press, 1995.

Powell, Mark Allan. *Giving to God: The Bible's Good News about Living a Generous Life*. Grand Rapids: Wm. B. Eerdmans Publishing, 2006.

Sacks, Jonathon. *To Heal a Fractured World: The Ethics of Responsibility*. New York: Schocken Books, 2007.

Salamon, Julie. *Rambam's Ladder: A Meditation on Generosity and Why It Is Necessary to Give*. New York: Workman Publishing Company, 2003.

Schneider, John R. *The Good of Affluence: Seeking God in a Culture of Wealth*. Grand Rapids: Wm. B. Eerdmans Publishing, 2002.

Schweiker, William, and Charles Matthews, eds. *Having: Property and Possession in Religious and Social Life.* Grand Rapids: Wm. B. Eerdmans Publishing, 2004.

Scott, Anthony, ed. *Good and Faithful Servant: Stewardship in the Orthodox Church.* Crestwood: St. Vladimir's Seminary Press, 2004.

Sider, Ronald J. *Rich Christians in an Age of Hunger: Moving from Affluence to Generosity.* Nashville: Thomas Nelson, 2005.

Toycen, Dave. *The Power of Generosity: How to Transform Yourself and Your World.* Waynesboro: Authentic Media, 2004.

Vallet, Ronald E. *Stepping Stones of the Steward: A Faith Journey through Jesus' Parables.* Grand Rapids: Wm. B. Eerdmans Publishing, 1994.

Vincent, Mark. *A Christian View of Money: Celebrating God's Generosity.* Eugene: Scottdale: Herald Press 1997.

Volf, Miroslav. *Free of Charge: Giving and Forgiving in a Culture Stripped of Grace.* Grand Rapids: Zondervan, 2006.

Wallis, Jim. "Spiritual Values and Economic Justice: When Did Jesus Become Pro-Rich?" In *God's Politics: Why the Right Gets it Wrong and the Left Doesn't Get It.* New York: HarperCollins, 2006, 209-97.

Wheeler, Sondra Ely. *Wealth as Peril and Obligation: The New Testament on Possessions.* Grand Rapids: Wm. B. Eerdmans Publishing, 1995.

Willmer, Wesley. *God and Your Stuff: The Vital Link between Your Possessions and Your Soul.* Colorado Springs: NavPress, 2002.

Zevit, Shawn Israel. *Offerings of the Heart: Money and Values in Faith Communities.* Herndon: Alban Institute, 2005.

SECULAR GIVING

Brown, Melissa S. ed. *Giving USA 2006: The Annual Report on Philanthropy for the Year 2005.* Glenview: Giving USA Foundation, 2006.

Burlingame, Dwight F., ed. *Philanthropy in America: A Comprehensive Historical Encyclopedia.* Santa Barbara: ABC-CLIO, 2004.

Clinton, Bill. *Giving: How Each of Us Can Change the World.* New York: Alfred A. Knopf, 2007.

Frumkin, Peter. *Strategic Giving: The Art and Science of Philanthropy.* Chicago: University of Chicago Press, 2006.

Guadiani, Claire. *The Greater Good: How Philanthropy Drives the American Economy and Can Save Capitalism.* New York: Holt Paperbacks, 2004.

Hamilton, Charles H., and Warren F. Ilchman, eds. "Cultures of Giving: How Region and Religion Influence Philanthropy." *New Directions for Philanthropic Fund-raising* Hoboken: Wiley, John and Sons, 1999.

Payton, Robert L. "God and Money." In *The Responsibilities of Wealth*, edited by Dwight F. Burlingame. Bloomington: Indiana University Press, 1992, 138–44.

Smith, David H., ed. *Good Intentions: Moral Obstacles and Opportunities.* Bloomington: Indiana University Press, 2005.

Wuthnow, Robert. *Acts of Compassion: Caring for Others and Helping Ourselves.* Princeton: Princeton University Press, 1993.

INSPIRATIONAL/SPIRITUAL VIEWS ON GIVING

Mallon, Theodore J. *The Journey toward Masterful Philanthropy.* Boulder: Five Centuries Press, 2004.

Ryan, M. J. *The Giving Heart: Unlocking the Transformative Power of Generosity in Your Life.* Berkeley: Conari Press, 2000.

DESCRIPTIVE ANALYSIS OF FAITH, MONEY, AND GIVING (RESEARCH AND ANALYSIS OF SURVEY DATA ON GIVING PATTERNS)

Brooks, Arthur. "Religious Faith and Charitable Giving," *Policy Review* 121 (October/November 2003).

Chaves, Mark, and Sharon L. Miller, eds. *Financing American Religion.* Walnut Creek: AltaMira Press, 1998.

Hoge, Dean, Charles Zech, Patrick McNamara, and Michael J. Donahue. *Money Matters: Personal Giving in American Churches.* Louisville: Westminster John Knox Press, 1996.

———. *Plain Talk about Churches and Money.* Herndon: Alban Institute, 1997.

Independent Sector. "Faith and Philanthropy: The Connection Between Charitable Behavior and Giving to Religion." *Giving and Volunteering in the United States.* Washington: Independent Sector, 2002.

Ronsvalle, John, and Sylvia Ronsvalle. *The State of Church Giving through 2004: Will We Will?* 16th ed. Champaign: Empty Tomb, 2006.

Wuthnow, Robert. *The Crisis in the Churches: Spiritual Malaise, Fiscal Woe*. New York: Oxford University Press, 1997.

———. *God and Mammon in America*. New York: New York Free Press, 1998.

———, ed. *Rethinking Materialism: Perspectives on the Spiritual Dimension of Economic Behavior*. Grand Rapids: Wm. B. Eerdmans Publishing, 1995.

Wuthnow, Robert, and Virginia A. Hodgkinson, eds. *Faith and Philanthropy in America: Exploring the Role of Religion in America's Voluntary Sector*. San Francisco: Jossey-Bass, 1990.

PROSCRIPTIVE ANALYSIS OF FAITH, MONEY, AND GIVING (PRACTICES OF FAITH COMMUNITIES, HOW CLERGY HANDLE MONEY, RELIGIOUS FUNDRAISING)

Conway, Daniel, ed. *The Reluctant Steward: A Report and Commentary on the Stewardship Development Study*. St. Meinrad: St. Meinrad School of Theology, 1992.

———. ed. *The Reluctant Steward Revisited: Preparing Pastors for Administrative and Financial Duties*. Indiana: St. Meinrad School of Theology, 2002.

Durall, Michael. *Creating Congregations of Generous People*. Herndon: Alban Institute, 1999.

Jeavons, Thomas H., and Rebekah Burch Basinger. *Growing Givers' Hearts: Treating Fund-raising as a Ministry*. San Francisco: Jossey-Bass, 2000.

Ronsvalle, John, and Sylvia Ronsvalle. *Behind the Stained Glass Windows: Money Dynamics in the Church*. Grand Rapids: Baker Books, 1996.

READINGS (COLLECTIONS, FICTION, MEMOIRS, QUOTES, PRIMARY TEXTS)

Blanchard, Ken, and S. Truett Cathy. *The Generosity Factor: Discover the Joy of Giving Your Time, Talent and Treasure*. Grand Rapids: Zondervan. 2002.

Carnegie, Andrew. *The Gospel of Wealth*. Reprinted by Dwight F. Burlingame, in *The Responsibilities of Wealth*. Bloomington: Indiana University Press, 1992, pp. 1–31.

Kass, Amy, ed. *The Perfect Gift: The Philanthropic Imagination in Poetry and Prose*. Indianapolis: University of Indianapolis Press, 2002.

Kittredge, William. *The Nature of Generosity*. New York: Vintage Books, 2001.

Powell, Michael. *A Thousand Paths to Generosity*. London: MQ Publications, 2004.

RESOURCES

ORGANIZATIONS THAT TEACH ABOUT THE PRACTICE OF GIVING

I recommend the following organizations if you are interested in learning more about giving as a sacred art.

DON'T ALMOST GIVE

Public Service Advisements (PSAs) campaign, guided by the Advertising Council and part of the Generous Nation campaign, http://www.dontalmostgive.org.

GOOD $ENSE MINISTRY — WILLOW CREEK ASSOCIATION

Empowers church leaders to implement a biblically based stewardship ministry within the local church.
PO Box 3188
Barrington, IL 60011-3188
800-570-9812
http://www.goodsenseministry.com

INTERNATIONAL CATHOLIC STEWARDSHIP COUNCIL

Promoting the concept of Christian stewardship.
1275 K Street, North West, Suite 880
Washington, DC 20005-4077
800-352-3452
http://www.catholicstewardship.org

LAKE INSTITUTE ON FAITH & GIVING

Offers a public forum for exploring the connections between individual philanthropy and faith and fosters a greater understanding of the ways in which faith both inspires and informs giving.
550 West North Street Suite 301
Indianapolis, IN 46202-3272
317-274-4200
http://www.philanthropy.iupui.edu/LakeFamilyInstitute

NATIONAL CENTER FOR BLACK PHILANTHROPY, INC.

Promotes and strengthens African American participation in all aspects of modern philanthropy.
1313 L Street, NW Suite 110
Washington, DC 20005
866-999-1700
http://www.ncfbp.net

NATIVE AMERICANS IN PHILANTHROPY

Promotes, facilitates, and celebrates philanthropic giving to Native communities from both Native and non-Native donors.
2801 21st Avenue South, Suite 132D
Minneapolis, MN 55407
612-724-8798
http://www.nativephilanthropy.org

THE PHILANTHROPY PROGRAM AT THE CENTER FOR CONTEMPLATIVE MIND IN SOCIETY

Explores ways to deepen and integrate what philanthropists value most in their inner lives with what they value most in their philanthropic work.
199 Main Street, Suite 3
Northampton, MA 01060
413-582-0071
http://www.contemplativemind.org/programs/philanthropy

THE PROJECT ON CIVIC REFLECTION

Helps civic groups build capacity, commitment and community through reading and discussion.
1401 Linwood Avenue
Valparaiso University
Valparaiso, IN 46383
219-464-6767
http://www.civicreflection.org

SHARE, SAVE, SPEND

Helping youth and adults achieve Financial Sanity™ by developing and maintaining healthy money habits.
Minneapolis, MN 55458
612-341-9996
http://www.sharesavespend.com

STEWARDSHIP CENTER

Serves Christian denominations, institutions, organizations, and congregations in developing creative and vital stewardship ministries.
1100 West 42nd Street Suite 225
Indianapolis, IN 46208-3304
800-835-5671
http://www.stewardshipresources.org

TENS — THE EPISCOPAL NETWORK FOR STEWARDSHIP

Transforming lives by developing a network of church leaders who encourage generosity.
345 S. Hydraulic
Wichita, KS 67211
800-699-2669
http://www.tens.org

TZEDAKAH, INC.

Helps raise the level and effectiveness of Jewish charitable giving by encouraging informed giving, accountability and openness within charitable organizations.
PO Box 34841
Bethesda MD 20827
301-299-7655
http://www.just-tzedakah.org

ZAKAT FOUNDATION OF AMERICA

International charity which aims to foster charitable giving and help generous and caring people reach out to those in need with direct aid.
P.O. Box 639
Worth, IL 60482
708-233-0555
http://www.thezakat.org

ORGANIZATIONS THAT GIVE OPPORTUNITIES TO PRACTICE GIVING

I recommend the following non-profit organizations, which offer a variety of ways to practice giving. This is not an exhaustive record of all "worthy" charities; rather, it is a list of organizations that I think represent the wide range of opportunities that exist. Moreover, I've included these charities because of the creative ways they offer to serve.

AMERICAN JEWISH WORLD SERVICE

An international development organization motivated by Judaism's imperative to pursue justice, dedicated to alleviating poverty, hunger, and disease among the people of the developing world regardless of race, religion, or nationality.
45 West 36th Street
New York, NY 10018
800-889-7146
http://www.AJWS.org

DELTA SOCIETY'S PET PARTNERS

Provides comprehensive training in animal-assisted activities and therapy to volunteers and health care professionals.
875 124th Ave NE Suite 101
Bellevue, WA 98005-2531
425-679-5500
http://www.deltasociety.org

DONORSCHOOSE.ORG

A website connecting classrooms in need with individuals who want to help, dedicated to addressing the issues of scarcity and inequitable distribution of learning materials and experiences in our public schools.
347 West 36th Street, Suite 503
New York, NY 10018
212-239-3615
http://www.donorschoose.org

DRESS FOR SUCCESS WORLDWIDE

Promotes the economic independence of disadvantaged women by providing professional attire, a network of support and the career development tools to help women thrive in work and in life.
32 East 31st Street
7th Floor
New York, NY 10016
212-532-1922
http://www.dressforsuccess.org

GLOBAL VOLUNTEERS

Private non-profit nonsectarian international development organization working for peace and mutual understanding between people of diverse cultures through the coordination of short-term volunteers, sometimes known as "volunteer vacations."
375 East Little Canada Road
St. Paul, MN 55117-1628
800-487-1074
http://www.globalvolunteers.org

THE I DO FOUNDATION

Links engaged couples with a host of charitable giving options for their wedding.
1133 19th Street NW, 9th Floor
Washington, DC 20036
202-736-5721
http://www.idofoundation.org

IGIVE

Shop online at over 680 brand name stores and a portion of each purchase will be donated to your favorite cause.
2859 Central Avenue
PMB 115
Evanston, IL 60201
800-372-6095
http://www.igive.com

KIVA

Connects people by allowing donors to make loans to the working poor in order to alleviate poverty.
3180 18th Street, Suite 201
San Francisco, CA 94110
888-445-5032
http://www.kiva.org

LOCKS OF LOVE

Provides hairpieces made from donated hair to financially disadvantaged children under age 18 who suffer from long-term medical hair loss.
2925 10th Avenue N Suite 102
Lake Worth, FL 33461-3099
888-896-1588
http://www.locksoflove.org

MAKING MEMORIES FOUNDATION

Grants wishes for metastatic breast cancer patients while continuing to support, educate, and increase resource awareness; famous for collecting wedding gowns and reselling them to collect money.
Making Memories Foundation
12708 SE Stephens Street
Portland, OR 97233
503-829-4486
http://www.makingmemories.org

ORGANIZATIONS THAT LEAD AND FACILITATE THE NON-PROFIT SECTOR

I recommend the following organizations if you are interested in learning more about philanthropy or the non-profit sector.

CENTER ON PHILANTHROPY AT INDIANA UNIVERSITY

An academic center that increases the understanding of philanthropy and improves its practice through teaching, research, public service, and public affairs activities throughout the world.
550 West North Street, Suite 301
Indianapolis, IN 46202
317-274-4200
http://www.philanthropy.iupui.edu

CHRONICLE ON PHILANTHROPY

The newspaper of the nonprofit world.
1255 23rd St. N.W. Suite 700
Washington, D.C. 20037
202-466-1200
http://www.philanthropy.com

INDEPENDENT SECTOR

Serves as the premier meeting ground for the leaders of America's charitable and philanthropic sector.
1200 Eighteenth Street, NW, Suite 200
Washington, DC 20036
202-467-6100
http://www.independentsector.org

CHARITY DATABASES

AMERICAN INSTITUTE OF PHILANTHROPY

Nonprofit charity watchdog and information service, providing donors with the information they need to make more informed giving decisions.
P.O. Box 578460
Chicago, IL 60657-8460
773-529-2300
http://www.charitywatch.org

CHARITY NAVIGATOR

Independent charity evaluator, working to advance a more efficient and responsive philanthropic marketplace by evaluating the financial health of over 5,300 of America's largest charities.
1200 MacArthur Boulevard, Second Floor
Mahwah, New Jersey 07430
201-818-1288
http://www.charitynavigator.org

GUIDESTAR

Database of information for over 1.7 million nonprofit organizations.
4801 Courthouse Street Suite 220
Williamsburg, VA 23188
757-229-4631
http://www.guidestar.org

NETWORK FOR GOOD

Locate volunteer opportunities by zip code; find and make a donation to a non-profit organization; get resources for your non-profit.
7920 Norfolk Avenue Suite 520
Bethesda, MD 20814
1-866-650-4636
http://www.helping.org

VOLUNTEERMATCH

Helps volunteers find a place to serve, and helps organizations find volunteers.
717 California St., Second Floor
San Francisco, CA 94108
415-241-6868
http://www.volunteermatch.org

FEEDBACK

Your feedback and stories are always a welcome treat to any author. Do you have a story about sacred giving or information about an organization that you would like to share? What does the *sacred art of giving* mean to you? Visit http://www.laurentylerwright.org, and send your comments directly to the author for possible publication on the website.

ACKNOWLEDGMENTS

No writer writes alone. We may isolate ourselves for hours or days at a time to be quiet with our thoughts, waiting for a brainstorm or attempting to string together the best choice of words, but we never write alone. Always with us are the wisdom and ideas of those who have influenced our thinking, the voices of loved ones who believe in us, and the presence of individuals and communities who have shaped us into who we are. While this book may bear my name, it is the result and work of many people.

Furman Religion Department—thank you for pushing my understanding of God beyond a singular denominational construct and teaching me how faith and reason can coexist peacefully in my soul.

Duke Divinity community—thank you for teaching me what it means to recognize and care for the "other" and for forming my entire being to better encounter the sacred.

Christian—I experience God through you. You are more than my little brother, you are my inspiration.

Dad—you are truly my hero. Over and over you have modeled what it looks like to live a lifestyle of generosity. No daughter could be more proud of her daddy! Your little girl loves you big time.

Mom—because of the million and one hats you've worn for me over the past 29 years (pregnancy survivor, casserole guru, resident grammar and vocabulary scholar, 24/7 taxi service driver, cheerleader extraordinaire) I am where I am today. This book is a product of your giving to me as much as it is anything else.

SkyLight Paths—I don't think any of us would have guessed this book, once slated to take six months, would have lasted two years. But it was well worth the journey. Stuart M. Matlins, publisher, and Emily Wichland, vice president of Editorial and Production—thank you for your support throughout. Heidi Johnson, assistant editor—thank you for your willingness to jump into this project on the back end and put so much effort into getting the manuscript ready for print. Mark Ogilbee, project editor—you proved your remarkable skill as an editor time and again ... providing unbelievable patience, being gentle with your feedback, pushing me when I needed some tough love. You brought out the best in me as a writer. Although I don't think God plays favorites, I tend to believe there's an extra blessing or two for editors who work with first-time authors.

Brent—your daily support has made this project possible ... leaving me post-its, writing me "you can do it" cards, making me dinner, staying awake with me, taking care of the dog, making me laugh, bringing me coffee, backing up my computer, sitting by me while I wrote, caring for me when my body decided to revolt, providing inspiration when my mind was blank, surprising me with flowers, believing in me when I didn't. You created space for me to live into the person God created.

I am so honored to have been given the chance to write this book, and I give thanks to God for allowing me the opportunity. There are so many others who have made this book possible because they have had a profound impact on who I am: Gram, Ann, Brooke, Kristin, Sarah, Jamalyn, Ashley, Charles, Mildred, Scottie, Henry, Jane, Louise, Candi, Lauren, Kelly, Betsy, Alex, Matthew, Brian, Sarah, Kevin, Jen, Jessica, Mark, Jeff, Philip, Meg, Debra, Jamestown UMC, St. Luke's UMC, Angier UMC, KPBC/Grace, Center on Philanthropy, Summersalt, Concoxions, and Annie. Any errors in the book can be attributed to me (and I do welcome your feedback), but everything else can be attributed to the influence of others as I have walked the journey of life and faith. To you all—thank you.

AVAILABLE FROM BETTER BOOKSTORES. TRY YOUR BOOKSTORE FIRST.

Global Spiritual Perspectives

Spiritual Perspectives on America's Role as Superpower
by the Editors at SkyLight Paths
Are we the world's good neighbor or a global bully? From a spiritual perspective, what are America's responsibilities as the only remaining superpower? Contributors:
Dr. Beatrice Bruteau • Dr. Joan Brown Campbell • Tony Campolo • Rev. Forrest Church • Lama Surya Das • Matthew Fox • Kabir Helminski • Thich Nhat Hanh • Eboo Patel • Abbot M. Basil Pennington, ocso • Dennis Prager • Rosemary Radford Ruether • Wayne Teasdale • Rev. William McD. Tully • Rabbi Arthur Waskow • John Wilson
5½ x 8½, 256 pp, Quality PB, 978-1-893361-81-2 **$16.95**

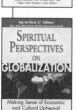

Spiritual Perspectives on Globalization, 2nd Edition
Making Sense of Economic and Cultural Upheaval
by Ira Rifkin; Foreword by Dr. David Little, Harvard Divinity School
What is globalization? Surveys the religious landscape. Includes a new Discussion Guide designed for group use.
5½ x 8½, 256 pp, Quality PB, 978-1-59473-045-0 **$16.99**

Hinduism / Vedanta

The Four Yogas
A Guide to the Spiritual Paths of Action, Devotion, Meditation and Knowledge
by Swami Adiswarananda
6 x 9, 320 pp, Quality PB, 978-1-59473-223-2 **$19.99**; HC, 978-1-59473-143-3 **$29.99**

Meditation & Its Practices
A Definitive Guide to Techniques and Traditions of Meditation in Yoga and Vedanta
by Swami Adiswarananda 6 x 9, 504 pp, Quality PB, 978-1-59473-105-1 **$24.99**

The Spiritual Quest and the Way of Yoga: The Goal, the Journey and the Milestones
by Swami Adiswarananda 6 x 9, 288 pp, HC, 978-1-59473-113-6 **$29.99**

Sri Ramakrishna, the Face of Silence
by Swami Nikhilananda and Dhan Gopal Mukerji
Edited with an Introduction by Swami Adiswarananda; Foreword by Dhan Gopal Mukerji II
Classic biographies present the life and thought of Sri Ramakrishna.
6 x 9, 352 pp, HC, 978-1-59473-115-0 **$29.99**

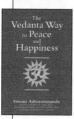

Sri Sarada Devi, The Holy Mother: Her Teachings and Conversations
Translated with Notes by Swami Nikhilananda; Edited with an Introduction by Swami Adiswarananda
6 x 9, 288 pp, HC, 978-1-59473-070-2 **$29.99**

The Vedanta Way to Peace and Happiness *by Swami Adiswarananda*
6 x 9, 240 pp, Quality PB, 978-1-59473-180-8 **$18.99**

Vivekananda, World Teacher: His Teachings on the Spiritual Unity of Humankind
Edited and with an Introduction by Swami Adiswarananda
6 x 9, 272 pp, Quality PB, 978-1-59473-210-2 **$21.99**

Sikhism

The First Sikh Spiritual Master
Timeless Wisdom from the Life and Teachings of Guru Nanak *by Harish Dhillon*
Tells the story of a unique spiritual leader who showed a gentle, peaceful path to God-realization while highlighting Guru Nanak's quest for tolerance and compassion. 6 x 9, 192 pp, Quality PB, 978-1-59473-209-6 **$16.99**

Or phone, fax, mail or e-mail to: SKYLIGHT PATHS Publishing
Sunset Farm Offices, Route 4 • P.O. Box 237 • Woodstock, Vermont 05091
Tel: (802) 457-4000 • Fax: (802) 457-4004 • www.skylightpaths.com
Credit card orders: (800) 962-4544 (8:30AM–5:30PM ET Monday–Friday)
Generous discounts on quantity orders. SATISFACTION GUARANTEED. Prices subject to change.

Children's Spirituality

ENDORSED BY CATHOLIC, PROTESTANT, JEWISH, AND BUDDHIST RELIGIOUS LEADERS

Adam and Eve's First Sunset: God's New Day
by Sandy Eisenberg Sasso; Full-color illus. by Joani Keller Rothenberg
9 x 12, 32 pp, Full-color illus., HC, 978-1-58023-177-0 **$17.95** *For ages 4 & up (a Jewish Lights book)*

Because Nothing Looks Like God
by Lawrence and Karen Kushner; Full-color illus. by Dawn W. Majewski
Real-life examples of happiness and sadness introduce children to the possibilities of spiritual life. 11 x 8½, 32 pp, HC, Full-color illus., 978-1-58023-092-6 **$17.99**
For ages 4 & up (a Jewish Lights book)
Also available: **Teacher's Guide,** 8½ x 11, 22 pp, PB, 978-1-58023-140-4 **$6.95** *For ages 5–8*

Becoming Me: A Story of Creation
by Martin Boroson; Full-color illus. by Christopher Gilvan-Cartwright
Told in the personal "voice" of the Creator, a story about creation and relationship that is about each one of us.
8 x 10, 32 pp, Full-color illus., HC, 978-1-893361-11-9 **$16.95** *For ages 4 & up*

But God Remembered: Stories of Women from Creation to the Promised Land
by Sandy Eisenberg Sasso; Full-color illus. by Bethanne Andersen
A fascinating collection of four different stories of women only briefly mentioned in biblical tradition and religious texts. 9 x 12, 32 pp, HC, Full-color illus., 978-1-879045-43-9 **$16.95**
For ages 8 & up (a Jewish Lights book)

Cain & Abel: Finding the Fruits of Peace
by Sandy Eisenberg Sasso; Full-color illus. by Joani Keller Rothenberg
A sensitive recasting of the ancient tale shows we have the power to deal with anger in positive ways. "Editor's Choice"—American Library Association's *Booklist*
9 x 12, 32 pp, HC, Full-color illus., 978-1-58023-123-7 **$16.95** *For ages 5 & up (a Jewish Lights book)*

Does God Hear My Prayer?
by August Gold; Full-color photos by Diane Hardy Waller
Introduces preschoolers and young readers to prayer and how it helps them express their own emotions. 10 x 8½, 32 pp, Quality PB, Full-color photo illus., 978-1-59473-102-0 **$8.99**

The 11th Commandment: Wisdom from Our Children *by The Children of America*
"If there were an Eleventh Commandment, what would it be?" Children of many religious denominations across America answer this question—in their own drawings and words. "A rare book of spiritual celebration for all people, of all ages, for all time." —*Bookviews*
8 x 10, 48 pp, HC, Full-color illus., 978-1-879045-46-0 **$16.95** *For all ages (a Jewish Lights book)*

For Heaven's Sake *by Sandy Eisenberg Sasso; Full-color illus. by Kathryn Kunz Finney*
Everyone talked about heaven: "Thank heavens." "Heaven forbid." "For heaven's sake, Isaiah." But no one would say what heaven was or how to find it. So Isaiah decides to find out, by seeking answers from many different people.
9 x 12, 32 pp, HC, Full-color illus., 978-1-58023-054-0 **$16.95** *For ages 4 & up (a Jewish Lights book)*

God in Between *by Sandy Eisenberg Sasso; Full-color illus. by Sally Sweetland*
A magical, mythical tale that teaches that God can be found where we are.
9 x 12, 32 pp, HC, Full-color illus., 978-1-879045-86-6 **$16.95** *For ages 4 & up (a Jewish Lights book)*

God's Paintbrush: Special 10th Anniversary Edition
Invites children of all faiths and backgrounds to encounter God through moments in their own lives. 11 x 8½, 32 pp, Full-color illus., HC, 978-1-58023-195-4 **$17.95** *For ages 4 & up*
Also available: **God's Paintbrush Teacher's Guide** 8½ x 11, 32 pp, PB, 978-1-879045-57-6 **$8.95**

God's Paintbrush Celebration Kit
A Spiritual Activity Kit for Teachers and Students of All Faiths, All Backgrounds
Additional activity sheets available:
8-Student Activity Sheet Pack (40 sheets/5 sessions), 978-1-58023-058-2 **$19.95**
Single-Student Activity Sheet Pack (5 sessions), 978-1-58023-059-9 **$3.95**

Children's Spirituality

ENDORSED BY CATHOLIC, PROTESTANT, JEWISH, AND BUDDHIST RELIGIOUS LEADERS

Remembering My Grandparent: A Kid's Own Grief Workbook in the Christian Tradition *by Nechama Liss-Levinson, PhD, and Rev. Molly Phinney Baskette, MDiv* 8 x 10, 48 pp, 2-color text, HC, 978-1-59473-212-6 **$16.99** *For ages 7–13*

Does God Ever Sleep? *by Joan Sauro, CSJ; Full-color photos*
A charming nighttime reminder that God is always present in our lives.
10 x 8½, 32 pp, Quality PB, Full-color photos, 978-1-59473-110-5 **$8.99** *For ages 3–6*

Does God Forgive Me? *by August Gold; Full-color photos by Diane Hardy Waller*
Gently shows how God forgives all that we do if we are truly sorry.
10 x 8½, 32 pp, Quality PB, Full-color photos, 978-1-59473-142-6 **$8.99** *For ages 3–6*

God Said Amen *by Sandy Eisenberg Sasso; Full-color illus. by Avi Katz*
A warm and inspiring tale of two kingdoms that shows us that we need only reach out to each other to find the answers to our prayers.
9 x 12, 32 pp, HC, Full-color illus., 978-1-58023-080-3 **$16.95**
For ages 4 & up (a Jewish Lights book)

How Does God Listen? *by Kay Lindahl; Full-color photos by Cynthia Maloney*
How do we know when God is listening to us? Children will find the answers to these questions as they engage their senses while the story unfolds, learning how God listens in the wind, waves, clouds, hot chocolate, perfume, our tears and our laughter.
10 x 8½, 32 pp, Quality PB, Full-color photos, 978-1-59473-084-9 **$8.99** *For ages 3–6*

In God's Hands *by Lawrence Kushner and Gary Schmidt; Full-color illus. by Matthew J. Baeck*
9 x 12, 32 pp, Full-color illus., HC, 978-1-58023-224-1 **$16.99** *For ages 5 & up (a Jewish Lights book)*

In God's Name *by Sandy Eisenberg Sasso; Full-color illus. by Phoebe Stone*
Like an ancient myth in its poetic text and vibrant illustrations, this award-winning modern fable about the search for God's name celebrates the diversity and, at the same time, the unity of all the people of the world.
9 x 12, 32 pp, HC, Full-color illus., 978-1-879045-26-2 **$16.99**
For ages 4 & up (a Jewish Lights book)

Also available in Spanish: **El nombre de Dios**
9 x 12, 32 pp, HC, Full-color illus., 978-1-893361-63-8 **$16.95**

In Our Image: God's First Creatures
by Nancy Sohn Swartz; Full-color illus. by Melanie Hall
A playful new twist on the Genesis story—from the perspective of the animals. Celebrates the interconnectedness of nature and the harmony of all living things.
9 x 12, 32 pp, HC, Full-color illus., 978-1-879045-99-6 **$16.95**
For ages 4 & up (a Jewish Lights book)

Noah's Wife: The Story of Naamah
by Sandy Eisenberg Sasso; Full-color illus. by Bethanne Andersen
This new story, based on an ancient text, opens readers' religious imaginations to new ideas about the well-known story of the Flood. When God tells Noah to bring the animals of the world onto the ark, God also calls on Naamah, Noah's wife, to save each plant on Earth.
9 x 12, 32 pp, HC, Full-color illus., 978-1-58023-134-3 **$16.95** *For ages 4 & up (a Jewish Lights book)*

Also available: **Naamah:** Noah's Wife (A Board Book)
by Sandy Eisenberg Sasso; Full-color illus. by Bethanne Andersen
5 x 5, 24 pp, Board Book, Full-color illus., 978-1-893361-56-0 **$7.99** *For ages 0–4*

Where Does God Live? *by August Gold and Matthew J. Perlman*
Using simple, everyday examples that children can relate to, this colorful book helps young readers develop a personal understanding of God.
10 x 8½, 32 pp, Quality PB, Full-color photo illus., 978-1-893361-39-3 **$8.99** *For ages 3–6*

Children's Spirituality—Board Books

Adam and Eve's New Day (A Board Book)
by Sandy Eisenberg Sasso; Full-color illus. by Joani Keller Rothenberg
A lesson in hope for every child who has worried about what comes next.
Abridged from *Adam and Eve's First Sunset*.
5 x 5, 24 pp, Full-color illus., Board Book, 978-1-59473-205-8 **$7.99** *For ages 0–4*

How Did the Animals Help God? (A Board Book)
by Nancy Sohn Swartz; Full-color illus. by Melanie Hall
Abridged from *In Our Image*, God asks all of nature to offer gifts to humankind—
with a promise that they will care for creation in return.
5 x 5, 24 pp, Board Book, Full-color illus., 978-1-59473-044-3 **$7.99** *For ages 0–4*

Where Is God? (A Board Book) *by Lawrence and Karen Kushner; Full-color illus. by
Dawn W. Majewski* A gentle way for young children to explore how God is with
us every day, in every way. Abridged from *Because Nothing Looks Like God*.
5 x 5, 24 pp, Board Book, Full-color illus., 978-1-893361-17-1 **$7.99** *For ages 0–4*

What Does God Look Like? (A Board Book)
by Lawrence and Karen Kushner; Full-color illus. by Dawn W. Majewski
A simple way for young children to explore the ways that we "see" God. Abridged
from *Because Nothing Looks Like God*.
5 x 5, 24 pp, Board Book, Full-color illus., 978-1-893361-23-2 **$7.99** *For ages 0–4*

How Does God Make Things Happen? (A Board Book)
by Lawrence and Karen Kushner; Full-color illus. by Dawn W. Majewski
A charming invitation for young children to explore how God makes things happen in
our world. Abridged from *Because Nothing Looks Like God*.
5 x 5, 24 pp, Board Book, Full-color illus., 978-1-893361-24-9 **$7.99** *For ages 0–4*

What Is God's Name? (A Board Book)
by Sandy Eisenberg Sasso; Full-color illus. by Phoebe Stone
Everyone and everything in the world has a name. What is God's name? Abridged
from the award-winning *In God's Name*.
5 x 5, 24 pp, Board Book, Full-color illus., 978-1-893361-10-2 **$7.99** *For ages 0–4*

What You Will See Inside ...

This important new series of books, each with many full-color photos, is designed to show children ages 6 and up the Who, What,
When, Where, Why and How of traditional houses of worship, liturgical celebrations, and rituals of different world faiths, empowering
them to respect and understand their own religious traditions—and
those of their friends and neighbors.

What You Will See Inside a Catholic Church
by Reverend Michael Keane; Foreword by Robert J. Keeley, EdD
Full-color photos by Aaron Pepis
8½ x 10½, 32 pp, Full-color photos, HC, 978-1-893361-54-6 **$17.95**

Also available in Spanish: **Lo que se puede ver dentro de una iglesia católica**
8½ x 10½, 32 pp, Full-color photos, HC, 978-1-893361-66-9 **$16.95**

What You Will See Inside a Hindu Temple
by Dr. Mahendra Jani and Dr. Vandana Jani; Full-color photos by Neirah Bhargava and Vijay Dave
8½ x 10½, 32 pp, Full-color photos, HC, 978-1-59473-116-7 **$17.99**

What You Will See Inside a Mosque
by Aisha Karen Khan; Full-color photos by Aaron Pepis
8½ x 10½, 32 pp, Full-color photos, HC, 978-1-893361-60-7 **$16.95**

What You Will See Inside a Synagogue
by Rabbi Lawrence A. Hoffman and Dr. Ron Wolfson; Full-color photos by Bill Aron
8½ x 10½, 32 pp, Full-color photos, HC, 978-1-59473-012-2 **$17.99**

Children's Spiritual Biography

Ten Amazing People
And How They Changed the World
by Maura D. Shaw; Foreword by Dr. Robert Coles
Full-color illus. by Stephen Marchesi

For ages 7 & up

Black Elk • Dorothy Day • Malcolm X • Mahatma Gandhi • Martin Luther King, Jr. • Mother Teresa • Janusz Korczak • Desmond Tutu • Thich Nhat Hanh • Albert Schweitzer

This vivid, inspirational and authoritative book will open new possibilities for children by telling the stories of how ten of the past century's greatest leaders changed the world in important ways.

8½ x 11, 48 pp, HC, Full-color illus., 978-1-893361-47-8 **$17.95**
For ages 7 & up

Spiritual Biographies for Young People—For ages 7 and up

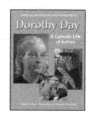
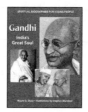
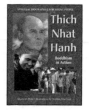

Black Elk: Native American Man of Spirit
by Maura D. Shaw; Full-color illus. by Stephen Marchesi
Through historically accurate illustrations and photos, inspiring age-appropriate activities and Black Elk's own words, this colorful biography introduces children to a remarkable person who ensured that the traditions and beliefs of his people would not be forgotten.
6¾ x 8¾, 32 pp, HC, Full-color and b/w illus., 978-1-59473-043-6 **$12.99**

Dorothy Day: A Catholic Life of Action
by Maura D. Shaw; Full-color illus. by Stephen Marchesi
Introduces children to one of the most inspiring women of the twentieth century, a down-to-earth spiritual leader who saw the presence of God in every person she met. Includes practical activities, a timeline and a list of important words to know.
6¾ x 8¾, 32 pp, HC, Full-color illus., 978-1-59473-011-5 **$12.99**

Gandhi: India's Great Soul
by Maura D. Shaw; Full-color illus. by Stephen Marchesi
There are a number of biographies of Gandhi written for young readers, but this is the only one that balances a simple text with illustrations, photographs, and activities that encourage children and adults to talk about how to make changes happen without violence. Introduces children to important concepts of freedom, equality and justice among people of all backgrounds and religions.
6¾ x 8¾, 32 pp, HC, Full-color illus., 978-1-893361-91-1 **$12.95**

Thich Nhat Hanh: Buddhism in Action
by Maura D. Shaw; Full-color illus. by Stephen Marchesi
Warm illustrations, photos, age-appropriate activities and Thich Nhat Hanh's own poems introduce a great man to children in a way they can understand and enjoy. Includes a list of important Buddhist words to know.
6¾ x 8¾, 32 pp, HC, Full-color illus., 978-1-893361-87-4 **$12.95**

Prayer / Meditation

Sacred Attention: A Spiritual Practice for Finding God in the Moment
by Margaret D. McGee
Framed on the Christian liturgical year, this inspiring guide explores ways to develop a practice of attention as a means of talking—and listening—to God.
6 x 9, 144 pp, HC, 978-1-59473-232-4 **$19.99**

Women Pray: Voices through the Ages, from Many Faiths, Cultures and Traditions
Edited and with Introductions by Monica Furlong
5 x 7¼, 256 pp, Quality PB, 978-1-59473-071-9 **$15.99**

Women of Color Pray: Voices of Strength, Faith, Healing, Hope and Courage *Edited and with Introductions by Christal M. Jackson*
Through these prayers, poetry, lyrics, meditations and affirmations, you will share in the strong and undeniable connection women of color share with God.
5 x 7¼, 208 pp, Quality PB, 978-1-59473-077-1 **$15.99**

Secrets of Prayer: A Multifaith Guide to Creating Personal Prayer in Your Life *by Nancy Corcoran, CSJ*
This compelling, multifaith guidebook offers you companionship and encouragement on the journey to a healthy prayer life. 6 x 9, 160 pp, Quality PB, 978-1-59473-215-7 **$16.99**

Prayers to an Evolutionary God
by William Cleary; Afterword by Diarmuid O'Murchu
Inspired by the spiritual and scientific teachings of Diarmuid O'Murchu and Teilhard de Chardin, reveals that religion and science can be combined to create an expanding view of the universe—an evolutionary faith.
6 x 9, 208 pp, HC, 978-1-59473-006-1 **$21.99**

The Art of Public Prayer: Not for Clergy Only   *by Lawrence A. Hoffman*
6 x 9, 288 pp, Quality PB, 978-1-893361-06-5 **$18.99**

A Heart of Stillness: A Complete Guide to Learning the Art of Meditation
by David A. Cooper 5½ x 8½, 272 pp, Quality PB, 978-1-893361-03-4 **$16.95**

Meditation without Gurus: A Guide to the Heart of Practice
by Clark Strand 5½ x 8½, 192 pp, Quality PB, 978-1-893361-93-5 **$16.95**

Praying with Our Hands: 21 Practices of Embodied Prayer from the World's
Spiritual Traditions *by Jon M. Sweeney; Photographs by Jennifer J. Wilson; Foreword by Mother Tessa Bielecki; Afterword by Taitetsu Unno, PhD*
8 x 8, 96 pp, 22 duotone photos, Quality PB, 978-1-893361-16-4 **$16.95**

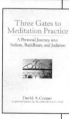

Silence, Simplicity & Solitude: A Complete Guide to Spiritual Retreat at Home
by David A. Cooper 5½ x 8½, 336 pp, Quality PB, 978-1-893361-04-1 **$16.95**

Three Gates to Meditation Practice: A Personal Journey into Sufism, Buddhism, and Judaism *by David A. Cooper* 5½ x 8½, 240 pp, Quality PB, 978-1-893361-22-5 **$16.95**

Prayer / M. Basil Pennington, OCSO

Finding Grace at the Center, 3rd Ed.: The Beginning of Centering Prayer *with Thomas Keating, OCSO, and Thomas E. Clarke, SJ; Foreword by Rev. Cynthia Bourgeault, PhD*
A practical guide to a simple and beautiful form of meditative prayer.
5 x 7¼, 128 pp, Quality PB, 978-1-59473-182-2 **$12.99**

The Monks of Mount Athos: A Western Monk's Extraordinary Spiritual Journey on Eastern Holy Ground *Foreword by Archimandrite Dionysios*
Explores the landscape, the monastic communities, and the food of Athos.
6 x 9, 256 pp, 10+ b/w drawings, Quality PB, 978-1-893361-78-2 **$18.95**

Psalms: A Spiritual Commentary *Illustrations by Phillip Ratner*
Reflections on some of the most beloved passages from the Bible's most widely read book.   6 x 9, 176 pp, 24 full-page b/w illus., Quality PB, 978-1-59473-234-8 **$16.99**
HC, 978-1-59473-141-9 **$19.99**

The Song of Songs: A Spiritual Commentary *Illustrations by Phillip Ratner*
Explore the Bible's most challenging mystical text.
6 x 9, 160 pp, 14 b/w illus., Quality PB, 978-1-59473-235-3 **$16.99**; HC, 978-1-59473-004-7 **$19.99**

Spiritual Poetry—The Mystic Poets

Experience these mystic poets as you never have before. Each beautiful, compact book includes: a brief introduction to the poet's time and place; a summary of the major themes of the poet's mysticism and religious tradition; essential selections from the poet's most important works; and an appreciative preface by a contemporary spiritual writer.

Hafiz
The Mystic Poets
Preface by Ibrahim Gamard
Hafiz is known throughout the world as Persia's greatest poet, with sales of his poems in Iran today only surpassed by those of the Qur'an itself. His probing and joyful verse speaks to people from all backgrounds who long to taste and feel divine love and experience harmony with all living things.
5 x 7¼, 144 pp, HC, 978-1-59473-009-2 **$16.99**

Hopkins
The Mystic Poets
Preface by Rev. Thomas Ryan, CSP
Gerard Manley Hopkins, Christian mystical poet, is beloved for his use of fresh language and startling metaphors to describe the world around him. Although his verse is lovely, beneath the surface lies a searching soul, wrestling with and yearning for God.
5 x 7¼, 112 pp, HC, 978-1-59473-010-8 **$16.99**

Tagore
The Mystic Poets
Preface by Swami Adiswarananda
Rabindranath Tagore is often considered the "Shakespeare" of modern India. A great mystic, Tagore was the teacher of W. B. Yeats and Robert Frost, the close friend of Albert Einstein and Mahatma Gandhi, and the winner of the Nobel Prize for Literature. This beautiful sampling of Tagore's two most important works, *The Gardener* and *Gitanjali,* offers a glimpse into his spiritual vision that has inspired people around the world.
5 x 7¼, 144 pp, HC, 978-1-59473-008-5 **$16.99**

Whitman
The Mystic Poets
Preface by Gary David Comstock
Walt Whitman was the most innovative and influential poet of the nineteenth century. This beautiful sampling of Whitman's most important poetry from *Leaves of Grass,* and selections from his prose writings, offers a glimpse into the spiritual side of his most radical themes—love for country, love for others, and love of Self.
5 x 7¼, 192 pp, HC, 978-1-59473-041-2 **$16.99**

Journeys of Simplicity
Traveling Light with Thomas Merton, Bashō, Edward Abbey, Annie Dillard & Others
Invites you to consider a more graceful way of traveling through life. Use the included journal pages (in PB only) to help you get started on your own spiritual journey.

Ed. by Philip Harnden
5 x 7¼, 144 pp, Quality PB, 978-1-59473-181-5 **$12.99**
128 pp, HC, 978-1-893361-76-8 **$16.95**

Sacred Texts—SkyLight Illuminations Series

Offers today's spiritual seeker an accessible entry into the great classic texts of the world's spiritual traditions. Each classic is presented in an accessible translation, with facing pages of guided commentary from experts, giving you the keys you need to understand the history, context and meaning of the text. This series enables you, whatever your background, to experience and understand classic spiritual texts directly, and to make them a part of your life.

CHRISTIANITY

The End of Days: Essential Selections from Apocalyptic Texts—
Annotated & Explained *Annotation by Robert G. Clouse*
Helps you understand the complex Christian visions of the end of the world.
5½ x 8½, 224 pp, Quality PB, 978-1-59473-170-9 **$16.99**

The Hidden Gospel of Matthew: Annotated & Explained
Translation & Annotation by Ron Miller
Takes you deep into the text cherished around the world to discover the words and events that have the strongest connection to the historical Jesus.
5½ x 8½, 272 pp, Quality PB, 978-1-59473-038-2 **$16.99**

The Lost Sayings of Jesus: Teachings from Ancient Christian, Jewish, Gnostic and Islamic Sources—Annotated & Explained
Translation & Annotation by Andrew Phillip Smith; Foreword by Stephan A. Hoeller
This collection of more than three hundred sayings depicts Jesus as a Wisdom teacher who speaks to people of all faiths as a mystic and spiritual master.
5½ x 8½, 240 pp, Quality PB, 978-1-59473-172-3 **$16.99**

Philokalia: The Eastern Christian Spiritual Texts—Selections Annotated & Explained *Annotation by Allyne Smith; Translation by G. E. H. Palmer, Phillip Sherrard and Bishop Kallistos Ware*
The first approachable introduction to the wisdom of the Philokalia, which is the classic text of Eastern Christian spirituality.
5½ x 8½, 240 pp, Quality PB, 978-1-59473-103-7 **$16.99**

The Sacred Writings of Paul: Selections Annotated & Explained
Translation & Annotation by Ron Miller
Explores the apostle Paul's core message of spiritual equality, freedom and joy.
5½ x 8½, 224 pp, Quality PB, 978-1-59473-213-3 **$16.99**

Sex Texts from the Bible: Selections Annotated & Explained
Translation & Annotation by Teresa J. Hornsby; Foreword by Amy-Jill Levine
Offers surprising insight into our modern sexual lives.
5½ x 8½, 208 pp, Quality PB, 978-1-59473-217-1 **$16.99**

Spiritual Writings on Mary: Annotated & Explained
Annotation by Mary Ford-Grabowsky; Foreword by Andrew Harvey
Examines the role of Mary, the mother of Jesus, as a source of inspiration in history and in life today. 5½ x 8½, 288 pp, Quality PB, 978-1-59473-001-6 **$16.99**

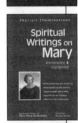

The Way of a Pilgrim: The Jesus Prayer Journey—Annotated & Explained
Translation & Annotation by Gleb Pokrovsky; Foreword by Andrew Harvey
This classic of Russian spirituality is the delightful account of one man who sets out to learn the prayer of the heart, also known as the "Jesus prayer."
5½ x 8½, 160 pp, Illus., Quality PB, 978-1-893361-31-7 **$14.95**

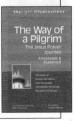

Sacred Texts—cont.

MORMONISM

The Book of Mormon: Selections Annotated & Explained
Annotation by Jana Riess; Foreword by Phyllis Tickle
Explores the sacred epic that is cherished by more than twelve million members of the LDS church as the keystone of their faith.
5½ x 8½, 272 pp, Quality PB, 978-1-59473-076-4 **$16.99**

NATIVE AMERICAN

Native American Stories of the Sacred: Annotated & Explained
Retold & Annotated by Evan T. Pritchard
Intended for more than entertainment, these teaching tales contain elegantly simple illustrations of time-honored truths.
5½ x 8½, 272 pp, Quality PB, 978-1-59473-112-9 **$16.99**

GNOSTICISM

Gnostic Writings on the Soul: Annotated & Explained
Translation & Annotation by Andrew Phillip Smith; Foreword by Stephan A. Hoeller
Reveals the inspiring ways your soul can remember and return to its unique, divine purpose.
5½ x 8½, 144 pp, Quality PB, 978-1-59473-220-1 **$16.99**

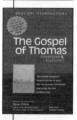

The Gospel of Philip: Annotated & Explained
Translation & Annotation by Andrew Phillip Smith; Foreword by Stevan Davies
Reveals otherwise unrecorded sayings of Jesus and fragments of Gnostic mythology.
5½ x 8½, 160 pp, Quality PB, 978-1-59473-111-2 **$16.99**

The Gospel of Thomas: Annotated & Explained
Translation & Annotation by Stevan Davies Sheds new light on the origins of Christianity and portrays Jesus as a wisdom-loving sage.
5½ x 8½, 192 pp, Quality PB, 978-1-893361-45-4 **$16.99**

The Secret Book of John: The Gnostic Gospel—Annotated & Explained
Translation & Annotation by Stevan Davies The most significant and influential text of the ancient Gnostic religion.
5½ x 8½, 208 pp, Quality PB, 978-1-59473-082-5 **$16.99**

JUDAISM

The Divine Feminine in Biblical Wisdom Literature
Selections Annotated & Explained
Translation & Annotation by Rabbi Rami Shapiro; Foreword by Rev. Cynthia Bourgeault, PhD
Uses the Hebrew books of Psalms, Proverbs, Song of Songs, Ecclesiastes and Job, Wisdom literature and the Wisdom of Solomon to clarify who Wisdom is.
5½ x 8½, 240 pp, Quality PB, 978-1-59473-109-9 **$16.99**

Ethics of the Sages: Pirke Avot—Annotated & Explained
Translation & Annotation by Rabbi Rami Shapiro Clarifies the ethical teachings of the early Rabbis. 5½ x 8½, 192 pp, Quality PB, 978-1-59473-207-2 **$16.99**

Hasidic Tales: Annotated & Explained
Translation & Annotation by Rabbi Rami Shapiro
Introduces the legendary tales of the impassioned Hasidic rabbis, presenting them as stories rather than as parables. 5½ x 8½, 240 pp, Quality PB, 978-1-893361-86-7 **$16.95**

The Hebrew Prophets: Selections Annotated & Explained
Translation & Annotation by Rabbi Rami Shapiro; Foreword by Zalman M. Schachter-Shalomi
Focuses on the central themes covered by all the Hebrew prophets.
5½ x 8½, 224 pp, Quality PB, 978-1-59473-037-5 **$16.99**

Zohar: Annotated & Explained *Translation & Annotation by Daniel C. Matt*
The best-selling author of *The Essential Kabbalah* brings together in one place the most important teachings of the Zohar, the canonical text of Jewish mystical tradition.
5½ x 8½, 176 pp, Quality PB, 978-1-893361-51-5 **$15.99**

Sacred Texts—cont.

ISLAM

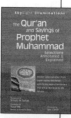

The Qur'an and Sayings of Prophet Muhammad
Selections Annotated & Explained
Annotation by Sohaib N. Sultan; Translation by Yusuf Ali; Revised by Sohaib N. Sultan
Foreword by Jane I. Smith
Explores how the timeless wisdom of the Qur'an can enrich your own spiritual journey.
5½ x 8½, 256 pp, Quality PB, 978-1-59473-222-5 **$16.99**

Rumi and Islam: Selections from His Stories, Poems, and Discourses—
Annotated & Explained
Translation & Annotation by Ibrahim Gamard
Focuses on Rumi's place within the Sufi tradition of Islam, providing insight into the mystical side of the religion.
5½ x 8½, 240 pp, Quality PB, 978-1-59473-002-3 **$15.99**

EASTERN RELIGIONS

The Art of War—Spirituality for Conflict
Annotated & Explained
by Sun Tzu; Annotation by Thomas Huynh; Translation by Thomas Huynh and the Editors at Sonshi.com; Foreword by Marc Benioff; Preface by Thomas Cleary
Highlights principles that encourage a perceptive and spiritual approach to conflict.
5½ x 8½, 256 pp, Quality PB, 978-1-59473-244-7 **$16.99**

Bhagavad Gita: Annotated & Explained
Translation by Shri Purohit Swami; Annotation by Kendra Crossen Burroughs
Explains references and philosophical terms, shares the interpretations of famous spiritual leaders and scholars, and more.
5½ x 8½, 192 pp, Quality PB, 978-1-893361-28-7 **$16.95**

Dhammapada: Annotated & Explained
Translation by Max Müller and revised by Jack Maguire; Annotation by Jack Maguire
Contains all of Buddhism's key teachings.
5½ x 8½, 160 pp, b/w photos, Quality PB, 978-1-893361-42-3 **$14.95**

Selections from the Gospel of Sri Ramakrishna
Annotated & Explained
Translation by Swami Nikhilananda; Annotation by Kendra Crossen Burroughs
Introduces the fascinating world of the Indian mystic and the universal appeal of his message.
5½ x 8½, 240 pp, b/w photos, Quality PB, 978-1-893361-46-1 **$16.95**

Tao Te Ching: Annotated & Explained
Translation & Annotation by Derek Lin; Foreword by Lama Surya Das
Introduces an Eastern classic in an accessible, poetic and completely original way.
5½ x 8½, 192 pp, Quality PB, 978-1-59473-204-1 **$16.99**

STOICISM

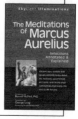

The Meditations of Marcus Aurelius
Selections Annotated & Explained
Annotation by Russell McNeil, PhD; Translation by George Long; Revised by Russell McNeil, PhD
Offers insightful and engaging commentary into the historical background of Stoicism.
5½ x 8½, 288 pp, Quality PB, 978-1-59473-236-2 **$16.99**

Spirituality of the Seasons

Autumn: A Spiritual Biography of the Season
Edited by Gary Schmidt and Susan M. Felch; Illustrations by Mary Azarian
Rejoice in autumn as a time of preparation and reflection. Includes Wendell Berry, David James Duncan, Robert Frost, A. Bartlett Giamatti, E. B. White, P. D. James, Julian of Norwich, Garret Keizer, Tracy Kidder, Anne Lamott, May Sarton.
6 x 9, 320 pp, 5 b/w illus., Quality PB, 978-1-59473-118-1 **$18.99**

Spring: A Spiritual Biography of the Season
Edited by Gary Schmidt and Susan M. Felch; Illustrations by Mary Azarian
Explore the gentle unfurling of spring and reflect on how nature celebrates rebirth and renewal. Includes Jane Kenyon, Lucy Larcom, Harry Thurston, Nathaniel Hawthorne, Noel Perrin, Annie Dillard, Martha Ballard, Barbara Kingsolver, Dorothy Wordsworth, Donald Hall, David Brill, Lionel Basney, Isak Dinesen, Paul Laurence Dunbar. 6 x 9, 352 pp, 6 b/w illus., Quality PB, 978-1-59473-246-1 **$18.99**

Summer: A Spiritual Biography of the Season
Edited by Gary Schmidt and Susan M. Felch; Illustrations by Barry Moser
"A sumptuous banquet.... These selections lift up an exquisite wholeness found within an everyday sophistication."— ★ *Publishers Weekly* starred review
Includes Anne Lamott, Luci Shaw, Ray Bradbury, Richard Selzer, Thomas Lynch, Walt Whitman, Carl Sandburg, Sherman Alexie, Madeleine L'Engle, Jamaica Kincaid.
6 x 9, 304 pp, 5 b/w illus., Quality PB, 978-1-59473-183-9 **$18.99**
HC, 978-1-59473-083-2 **$21.99**

Winter: A Spiritual Biography of the Season
Edited by Gary Schmidt and Susan M. Felch; Illustrations by Barry Moser
"This outstanding anthology features top-flight nature and spirituality writers on the fierce, inexorable season of winter.... Remarkably lively and warm, despite the icy subject." — ★ *Publishers Weekly* starred review
Includes Will Campbell, Rachel Carson, Annie Dillard, Donald Hall, Ron Hansen, Jane Kenyon, Jamaica Kincaid, Barry Lopez, Kathleen Norris, John Updike, E. B. White.
6 x 9, 288 pp, 6 b/w illus., Deluxe PB w/flaps, 978-1-893361-92-8 **$18.95**
HC, 978-1-893361-53-9 **$21.95**

Spirituality / Animal Companions

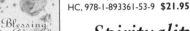

Blessing the Animals: Prayers and Ceremonies to Celebrate God's Creatures, Wild and Tame *Edited by Lynn L. Caruso* 5 x 7¼, 256 pp, HC, 978-1-59473-145-7 **$19.99**

Remembering My Pet: A Kid's Own Spiritual Workbook for When a Pet Dies
by Nechama Liss-Levinson, PhD, and Rev. Molly Phinney Baskette, MDiv; Foreword by Lynn L. Caruso
8 x 10, 48 pp, 2-color text, HC, 978-1-59473-221-3 **$16.99**

What Animals Can Teach Us about Spirituality: Inspiring Lessons from Wild and Tame Creatures *by Diana L. Guerrero* 6 x 9, 176 pp, Quality PB, 978-1-893361-84-3 **$16.95**

Spirituality—A Week Inside

Come and Sit: A Week Inside Meditation Centers
by Marcia Z. Nelson; Foreword by Wayne Teasdale
6 x 9, 224 pp, b/w photos, Quality PB, 978-1-893361-35-5 **$16.95**

Lighting the Lamp of Wisdom: A Week Inside a Yoga Ashram
by John Ittner; Foreword by Dr. David Frawley
6 x 9, 192 pp, 10+ b/w photos, Quality PB, 978-1-893361-52-2 **$15.95**

Making a Heart for God: A Week Inside a Catholic Monastery
by Dianne Aprile; Foreword by Brother Patrick Hart, OCSO
6 x 9, 224 pp, b/w photos, Quality PB, 978-1-893361-49-2 **$16.95**

Waking Up: A Week Inside a Zen Monastery
by Jack Maguire; Foreword by John Daido Loori, Roshi
6 x 9, 224 pp, b/w photos, Quality PB, 978-1-893361-55-3 **$16.95**; HC, 978-1-893361-13-3 **$21.95**

Spirituality

Next to Godliness: Finding the Sacred in Housekeeping
Edited and with Introductions by Alice Peck
Offers new perspectives on how we can reach out for the Divine.
6 x 9, 224 pp, Quality PB, 978-1-59473-214-0 **$19.99**

Bread, Body, Spirit: Finding the Sacred in Food
Edited and with Introductions by Alice Peck
Explores how food feeds our faith. 6 x 9, 224 pp, Quality PB, 978-1-59473-242-3 **$19.99**

Renewal in the Wilderness: A Spiritual Guide to Connecting with God in the Natural World *by John Lionberger*
Reveals the power of experiencing God's presence in many variations of the natural world. 6 x 9, 176 pp, b/w photos, Quality PB, 978-1-59473-219-5 **$16.99**

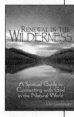

Honoring Motherhood: Prayers, Ceremonies and Blessings
Edited and with Introductions by Lynn L. Caruso
Journey through the seasons of motherhood. 5 x 7¼, 272 pp, HC, 978-1-59473-239-3 **$19.99**

Soul Fire: Accessing Your Creativity *by Rev. Thomas Ryan, CSP*
Learn to cultivate your creative spirit. 6 x 9, 160 pp, Quality PB, 978-1-59473-243-0 **$16.99**

Technology & Spirituality: How the Information Revolution Affects Our Spiritual Lives *by Stephen K. Spyker* 6 x 9, 176 pp, HC, 978-1-59473-218-8 **$19.99**

Money and the Way of Wisdom: Insights from the Book of Proverbs
by Timothy J. Sandoval, PhD 6 x 9, 192 pp (est), Quality PB, 978-1-59473-245-4 **$16.99**

Awakening the Spirit, Inspiring the Soul
30 Stories of Interspiritual Discovery in the Community of Faiths
Edited by Brother Wayne Teasdale and Martha Howard, MD; Foreword by Joan Borysenko, PhD
6 x 9, 224 pp, HC, 978-1-59473-039-9 **$21.99**

Creating a Spiritual Retirement: A Guide to the Unseen Possibilities in Our Lives
by Molly Srode 6 x 9, 208 pp, b/w photos, Quality PB, 978-1-59473-050-4 **$14.99**
HC, 978-1-893361-75-1 **$19.95**

Finding Hope: Cultivating God's Gift of a Hopeful Spirit
by Marcia Ford 8 x 8, 200 pp, Quality PB, 978-1-59473-211-9 **$16.99**

The Geography of Faith: Underground Conversations on Religious, Political and Social Change *by Daniel Berrigan and Robert Coles* 6 x 9, 224 pp, Quality PB, 978-1-893361-40-9 **$16.95**

Jewish Spirituality: A Brief Introduction for Christians *by Lawrence Kushner*
5½ x 8½, 112 pp, Quality PB, 978-1-58023-150-3 **$12.95** *(a Jewish Lights book)*

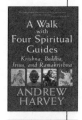

Journeys of Simplicity: Traveling Light with Thomas Merton, Bashō, Edward Abbey, Annie Dillard & Others *by Philip Harnden* 5 x 7¼, 144 pp, Quality PB, 978-1-59473-181-5 **$12.99** 128 pp, HC, 978-1-893361-76-8 **$16.95**

Keeping Spiritual Balance As We Grow Older: More than 65 Creative Ways to Use Purpose, Prayer, and the Power of Spirit to Build a Meaningful Retirement
by Molly and Bernie Srode 8 x 8, 224 pp, Quality PB, 978-1-59473-042-9 **$16.99**

Spirituality 101: The Indispensable Guide to Keeping—or Finding—Your Spiritual Life on Campus *by Harriet L. Schwartz, with contributions from college students at nearly thirty campuses across the United States* 6 x 9, 272 pp, Quality PB, 978-1-59473-000-9 **$16.99**

Spiritually Incorrect: Finding God in All the *Wrong* Places *by Dan Wakefield; Illus. by Marian DelVecchio* 5½ x 8½, 192 pp, b/w illus., Quality PB, 978-1-59473-137-2 **$15.99**

Spiritual Manifestos: Visions for Renewed Religious Life in America from Young Spiritual Leaders of Many Faiths *Edited by Niles Elliot Goldstein; Preface by Martin E. Marty*
6 x 9, 256 pp, HC, 978-1-893361-09-6 **$21.95**

A Walk with Four Spiritual Guides: Krishna, Buddha, Jesus, and Ramakrishna
by Andrew Harvey 5½ x 8½, 192 pp, 10 b/w photos & illus., Quality PB, 978-1-59473-138-9 **$15.99**

What Matters: Spiritual Nourishment for Head and Heart
by Frederick Franck 5 x 7¼, 128 pp, 50+ b/w illus., HC, 978-1-59473-013-9 **$16.99**

Who Is My God?, 2nd Edition: An Innovative Guide to Finding Your Spiritual Identity
Created by the Editors at SkyLight Paths 6 x 9, 160 pp, Quality PB, 978-1-59473-014-6 **$15.99**

Spirituality & Crafts

The Knitting Way
A Guide to Spiritual Self-Discovery
by Linda Skolnik and Janice MacDaniels
Examines how you can explore and strengthen your spiritual life through knitting.
7 x 9, 240 pp, Quality PB, b/w photographs, 978-1-59473-079-5 **$16.99**

The Scrapbooking Journey
A Hands-On Guide to Spiritual Discovery
by Cory Richardson-Lauve; Foreword by Stacy Julian
Reveals how this craft can become a practice used to deepen and shape your life.
7 x 9, 176 pp, Quality PB, 8-page full-color insert, plus b/w photographs
978-1-59473-216-4 **$18.99**

The Painting Path
Embodying Spiritual Discovery through Yoga, Brush and Color
by Linda Novick; Foreword by Richard Segalman
Explores the divine connection you can experience through creativity.
7 x 9, 208 pp, 8-page full-color insert, plus b/w photographs
Quality PB, 978-1-59473-226-3 **$18.99**

The Quilting Path
A Guide to Spiritual Discovery through Fabric, Thread and Kabbalah
by Louise Silk
Explores how to cultivate personal growth through quilt making.
7 x 9, 192 pp, Quality PB, b/w photographs and illustrations, 978-1-59473-206-5 **$16.99**

Contemplative Crochet
A Hands-On Guide for Interlocking Faith and Craft
by Cindy Crandall-Frazier; Foreword by Linda Skolnik
Illuminates the spiritual lessons you can learn through crocheting.
7 x 9, 192 pp (est), b/w photographs, Quality PB, 978-1-59473-238-6 **$16.99**

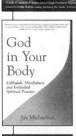

Kabbalah / Enneagram
(from Jewish Lights Publishing)

God in Your Body: Kabbalah, Mindfulness and Embodied Spiritual Practice
by Jay Michaelson 6 x 9, Quality PB Original, 978-1-58023-304-0 **$18.99**

Cast in God's Image: Discover Your Personality Type Using the Enneagram and Kabbalah
by Rabbi Howard A. Addison 7 x 9, 176 pp, Quality PB, 978-1-58023-124-4 **$16.95**

Ehyeh: A Kabbalah for Tomorrow *by Dr. Arthur Green*
6 x 9, 224 pp, Quality PB, 978-1-58023-213-5 **$16.99**

The Enneagram and Kabbalah, 2nd Edition: Reading Your Soul
by Rabbi Howard A. Addison 6 x 9, 192 pp, Quality PB, 978-1-58023-229-6 **$16.99**

The Gift of Kabbalah: Discovering the Secrets of Heaven, Renewing Your Life on Earth
by Tamar Frankiel, PhD 6 x 9, 256 pp, Quality PB, 978-1-58023-141-1 **$16.95**
HC, 978-1-58023-108-4 **$21.95**

Kabbalah: A Brief Introduction for Christians
by Tamar Frankiel, PhD 5½ x 8½, 176 pp, Quality PB, 978-1-58023-303-3 **$16.99**

Zohar: Annotated & Explained *Translation and Annotation by Dr. Daniel C. Matt*
Foreword by Andrew Harvey 5½ x 8½, 176 pp, Quality PB, 978-1-893361-51-5 **$15.99**
(a SkyLight Paths book)

Spiritual Practice

Soul Fire: Accessing Your Creativity by Rev. Thomas Ryan, CSP
Shows you how to cultivate your creative spirit as a way to encourage personal growth.
6 x 9, 160 pp, Quality PB, 978-1-59473-243-0 **$16.99**

Running—The Sacred Art: Preparing to Practice
by Dr. Warren A. Kay; Foreword by Kristin Armstrong
Examines how your daily run can enrich your spiritual life.
5½ x 8½, 160 pp, Quality PB, 978-1-59473-227-0 **$16.99**

Hospitality—The Sacred Art: Discovering the Hidden Spiritual Power
of Invitation and Welcome by Rev. Nanette Sawyer; Foreword by Rev. Dirk Ficca
Explores how this ancient spiritual practice can transform your relationships.
5½ x 8½, 192 pp, Quality PB, 978-1-59473-228-7 **$16.99**

Thanking & Blessing—The Sacred Art: Spiritual Vitality through
Gratefulness by Jay Marshall, PhD; Foreword by Philip Gulley
Offers practical tips for uncovering the blessed wonder in our lives—even in trying circumstances. 5½ x 8½, 176 pp, Quality PB, 978-1-59473-231-7 **$16.99**

Everyday Herbs in Spiritual Life: A Guide to Many Practices
by Michael J. Caduto; Foreword by Rosemary Gladstar Explores the power of herbs.
7 x 9, 208 pp, 21 b/w illustrations, Quality PB, 978-1-59473-174-7 **$16.99**

Divining the Body: Reclaim the Holiness of Your Physical Self by Jan Phillips
8 x 8, 256 pp, Quality PB, 978-1-59473-080-1 **$16.99**

Finding Time for the Timeless: Spirituality in the Workweek
by John McQuiston II Simple stories show you how refocus your daily life.
5½ x 6¾, 208 pp, HC, 978-1-59473-035-1 **$17.99**

The Gospel of Thomas: A Guidebook for Spiritual Practice
by Ron Miller; Translations by Stevan Davies
6 x 9, 160 pp, Quality PB, 978-1-59473-047-4 **$14.99**

Earth, Water, Fire, and Air: Essential Ways of Connecting to Spirit
by Cait Johnson 6 x 9, 224 pp, HC, 978-1-893361-65-2 **$19.95**

Labyrinths from the Outside In: Walking to Spiritual Insight—A Beginner's Guide
by Donna Schaper and Carole Ann Camp
6 x 9, 208 pp, b/w illus. and photos, Quality PB, 978-1-893361-18-8 **$16.95**

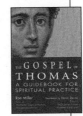

Practicing the Sacred Art of Listening: A Guide to Enrich Your Relationships
and Kindle Your Spiritual Life—The Listening Center Workshop
by Kay Lindahl 8 x 8, 176 pp, Quality PB, 978-1-893361-85-0 **$16.95**

Releasing the Creative Spirit: Unleash the Creativity in Your Life
by Dan Wakefield 7 x 10, 256 pp, Quality PB, 978-1-893361-36-2 **$16.95**

The Sacred Art of Bowing: Preparing to Practice
by Andi Young 5½ x 8½, 128 pp, b/w illus., Quality PB, 978-1-893361-82-9 **$14.95**

The Sacred Art of Chant: Preparing to Practice
by Ana Hernández 5½ x 8½, 192 pp, Quality PB, 978-1-59473-036-8 **$15.99**

The Sacred Art of Fasting: Preparing to Practice
by Thomas Ryan, CSP 5½ x 8½, 192 pp, Quality PB, 978-1-59473-078-8 **$15.99**

The Sacred Art of Forgiveness: Forgiving Ourselves and Others through God's Grace
by Marcia Ford 8 x 8, 176 pp, Quality PB, 978-1-59473-175-4 **$16.99**

The Sacred Art of Listening: Forty Reflections for Cultivating a Spiritual Practice
by Kay Lindahl; Illustrations by Amy Schnapper
8 x 8, 160 pp, b/w illus., Quality PB, 978-1-893361-44-7 **$16.99**

The Sacred Art of Lovingkindness: Preparing to Practice
by Rabbi Rami Shapiro; Foreword by Marcia Ford 5½ x 8½, 176 pp, Quality PB, 978-1-59473-151-8
$16.99

Sacred Speech: A Practical Guide for Keeping Spirit in Your Speech
by Rev. Donna Schaper 6 x 9, 176 pp, Quality PB, 978-1-59473-068-9 **$15.99**
HC, 978-1-893361-74-4 **$21.95**

AVAILABLE FROM BETTER BOOKSTORES.
TRY YOUR BOOKSTORE FIRST.

About SKYLIGHT PATHS Publishing

SkyLight Paths Publishing is creating a place where people of different spiritual traditions come together for challenge and inspiration, a place where we can help each other understand the mystery that lies at the heart of our existence.

Through spirituality, our religious beliefs are increasingly becoming a part of our lives—rather than *apart* from our lives. While many of us may be more interested than ever in spiritual growth, we may be less firmly planted in traditional religion. Yet, we do want to deepen our relationship to the sacred, to learn from our own as well as from other faith traditions, and to practice in new ways.

SkyLight Pa   **INFCW   205**   ity that increasingly transce   **.677**   ination—people
wanting to l   **W951**   *ie way.*

For your in   ; book we have
provided a   **WRIGHT, LAUREN TYLER,**   find interesting
and useful.   **GIVING, THE SACRED ART**

   Buddhisr   :ism
   Catholici   **CENTRAL LIBRARY**   m
   Children   **03/09**

Christianity	Hinduism /	Prayer
Comparative	Vedanta	Religious Etiquette
Religion	Inspiration	Retirement
Current Events	Islam / Sufism	Spiritual Biography
Earth-Based	Judaism	Spiritual Direction
Spirituality	Kabbalah	Spirituality
Enneagram	Meditation	Women's Interest
	Midrash Fiction	Worship

Or phone, fax, mail or e-mail to: SKYLIGHT PATHS Publishing
Sunset Farm Offices, Route 4 • P.O. Box 237 • Woodstock, Vermont 05091
Tel: (802) 457-4000 • Fax: (802) 457-4004 • www.skylightpaths.com
Credit card orders: (800) 962-4544 (8:30AM–5:30PM ET Monday–Friday)
Generous discounts on quantity orders. SATISFACTION GUARANTEED. Prices subject to change.

For more information about each book,
visit our website at www.skylightpaths.com